I0799482

The MARION POPCORN FESTIVAL

Michelle Rotuno-Johnson

The Marion Popcorn Festival

A Fun-Filled History

American Palate

Published by American Palate
A Division of The History Press
Charleston, SC 29403
www.historypress.net

First published 2014

Manufactured in the United States

ISBN 978.1.62619.661.2

Library of Congress CIP data applied for.

Notice: The information in this book is true and complete to the best of our knowledge. It is offered without guarantee on the part of the author or The History Press. The author and The History Press disclaim all liability in connection with the use of this book.

This book is dedicated to those of us who dream big.

CONTENTS

Contents

FOREWORD

During several gatherings at a local restaurant that included local entrepreneurs, the discussion led to what we felt was missing in Marion, Ohio, as far as events are concerned.

It was noted that a few years ago, Marion had a semipro baseball team, an indoor ice-skating rink at the coliseum and drum and bugle corps finals, along with other smaller events. A discussion ensued about what we as a group could do to shine the spotlight on the city of Marion.

It was determined that other cities, small and large, had introduced festivals related to their local foods, such as the Bratwurst Festival, the Pumpkin Festival, the Corn Festival, the Zucchini Festival and several others. Naturally, we had a difficult time determining what type of food festival we could start. The idea of a Popcorn Festival "popped" up since we have Wyandot Popcorn and other snacks manufactured right here in Marion.

Of course, many things had to be determined and take place, such as obtaining approval from the city, local police and fire departments, as well as local businesspeople. Fortunately, our little group had the right experience and connections to accomplish all these tasks. The group made several visits to other festivals and the Ohio State Fair promoting its forthcoming festival to their respective organizers and as many of the best food vendors as possible. The streets were then laid out to be blocked off as required. Several other ideas were brought up concerning insurance, entertainment, beer gardens and sponsorship. Beer gardens and sponsorships were to provide seed money for the production of the festival and for the free entertainment.

Foreword

The dates were set to be the first weekend after Labor Day due to the projected favorable weather conditions based on historical information from the *Farmer's Almanac*. Hence, the first Popcorn Festival started in September 1981. That first Popcorn Festival turned out to be a huge success thanks to the help of many, many volunteers, the water company, the electric company and others. The festival didn't make much money, but it didn't lose money either.

Once the opening ceremonies start, it has become tradition that the festival officers and most of the committee chairpersons gather backstage and celebrate another year of hard work with "shooters," then get back to work.

Although this is just a synopsis of how the festival got started, there have been many changes and additions, such as the numerous different events that go on throughout the year, including beauty pageants for the Miss Popcorn Festival, Tiny Pop, Wee Pop, the corn-shucking contest, the 5K run, the golf tournament, et cetera.

All in all, the Popcorn Festival has become one of the premier events in the state of Ohio.

Pat Regules, First Festival Director
with help from wife Kathy Regules, June 2014

ACKNOWLEDGEMENTS

This work would not have been possible without the time and energy of many other people who agreed to help me in this process. I don't think any number of words can express my gratitude to so many friends, family, acquaintances and colleagues.

Thank you to my editor, Greg Dumais, who e-mailed me in December 2013 and still wanted to do the project in February 2014 when I finally found his letter again in my unread e-mails and had the courtesy to e-mail him back. Thank you for your patience and encouragement—especially the patience part. Thank you also to the rest of the staff at The History Press for your work to make this book a reality.

Thank you to Gale Martin and the staff at the Marion County Historical Society/Wyandot Popcorn Museum for scanning photos, answering questions and being accessible as I chased this project. You have all been wonderfully helpful. I couldn't have done it without you! The binders full of popcorn knowledge (which I think Kathy Regules helped put together) and the website were so valuable to me.

Thank you to Mike Nicolosi, Phyllis Hendrix, Karen Herr, Karen Shaffer, Lynn Zucker, Pat Regules, Kathy Regules and Norma Castanien for the history lessons, your time, your input, your memories and your help. To Mark Schwartzkopf and any other festival experts who died before I sat down to write this, thank you as well. Thank you to Marion mayor Scott Schertzer and to Diane Watson, director of the Marion County Convention and Visitors' Bureau, for your insight on the festival's impact on Marion.

Acknowledgements

Thanks to Brooks Brown for your time and your memories, as well as the background information on Wyandot. A special thanks as well to the rest of the Brown family, especially George Brown, W. Hoover Brown and Ava (King) Brown, whose work and words helped shape this book.

Thank you to my Marion friends Delaney, Hank and Liz, who shared their memories of this fun festival with me. Hope to see you up there sometime.

I owe a huge debt to everyone who has ever encouraged my writing passion, from the room moms who helped me publish books in elementary school, to anyone who read the handwritten newspaper I passed around on Lindale Drive as a kid, to the people who read my fan fiction on the Internet.

Special thanks to Bill Carey, my high school English teacher at Roger Bacon. Thanks also to Joe Musser, Melinda Rhodes, Jim Underwood, Trace Regan and countless others I met at Ohio Wesleyan as I pursued my degrees. Thank you also to anyone who read my opinion columns in the school paper, particularly if I made you laugh or made you angry.

Thank you to Dave Willacker, who taught me the importance of a good handshake, a polite attitude and a strong work ethic, and to the rest of you at Cincinnati Circus Company.

Thank you to Kaitlin Thomas, the best big in the world, for supporting my crazy dreams and getting me to watch *Teen Wolf*. That has nothing to do with this book, but it is darn good television. For all my other Delta Zeta sisters, thank you for allowing me to hone my leadership skills with you in college and for your unwavering love.

Thanks to my other sisters in Capitol Showcase Chorus for your encouragement.

Thank you to my grandma Jo, who has always encouraged me to dream big and who is one of my biggest cheerleaders. Thank you to my mom and dad for allowing me to be a creative tomboy with a ton of Beanie Babies and books and for your love and support all these years. Thank you to my brothers, Matthew and Michael, for making me laugh and making me proud. I love you guys, and I can't wait to see what your lives have in store for you when you become "real, responsible adults" like your big sister.

Thank you to my fiancée, Leah, for your unconditional love and support and for listening to me talk about popcorn all the time. You are such an anchor for me and the best partner I could have asked for. You keep me grounded when my head is in the clouds. Isn't my dream of becoming an author better than the times I wanted to open a food truck or all the times I was convinced I would become a famous country singer? (I'm still waiting on that chance, by the way, if any record execs are reading this.)

Acknowledgements

Thank you to my colleagues in the newsroom who have helped me grow in a different style of writing and who keep me smiling in this crazy industry. Tom, Nick, James, Bill, Denny, John—you're all great reporters and fantastic men. Thank you for everything.

Thank you to the people of Marion who have helped me see the value of hard work and unflappable persistence.

And of course, I would be a fool if I didn't thank you, the person holding this book, for supporting me and supporting local history. I hope you enjoy it!

Introduction

A MARION TRADITION

The weekend after Labor Day every year, the streets of Marion, Ohio, shut down.

Food vendors and amusement ride operators roll into the central Ohio county. Some pass fields of corn and the tomb or home of President Warren G. Harding on their way to downtown Marion. And for a whole weekend, the county of sixty-seven thousand people plays host to the world's largest popcorn festival.

The Marion Popcorn Festival, founded in 1981 to celebrate Marion's contributions to the snack food industry, draws an estimated 200,000 to 250,000 people every year. As the festival has aged, it has become known more for the pageants and the national recording artists who grace the stage, but there are still popcorn vendors to be found.

The festival may well be one of the last weekends before fall sets in to savor funnel cakes, giant cheese steaks and lemonade shake-ups and then feel a little queasy on the Tilt-A-Whirl. Fashions have changed, vendors have come and gone, but the festival is still basically the same as it was in 1981.

Legal professionals and local business owners who work downtown will wander outside on Thursday and Friday to get lunch from one of the many concessionaires, and people will see old classmates they haven't seen in awhile—or at least since last year's festival.

People come from all over for the festival, and many show up for the entertainment that plays on the main stage. In 2013, disco group the Village People and country singer-songwriter Jo Dee Messina joined the halls of

This ride would be a perfect opportunity to see the whole festival—if you can keep your food in your stomach. *Marion Popcorn Festival.*

Young festival-goers get into the spirit of the festival. *Wyandot Popcorn Museum.*

Vendors stretch down Center Street at the Marion Popcorn Festival. *Marion Popcorn Festival.*

Popcorn Festival artists entertaining the masses for free. They packed the streets of Marion, much like Willie Nelson, Styx, Kansas, Blake Shelton, Boyz II Men and many others have done since 1981. The year 2014 will bring Night Ranger and Craig Morgan into the fold.

The Thursday evening parade also draws a major following, with many people setting out their chairs on the side of the street several days in advance. Local businesses, schools, churches, politicians and more will

Popcorn Festival Facts and Features

- The largest popcorn festival in the world
- Held annually the weekend after Labor Day in Marion, Ohio
- Founded in 1981 to celebrate the county's popcorn production history
- Estimated crowds of 200,000 to 250,000 a year
- Entertainment Thursday, Friday and Saturday nights
- Three-hundred-unit parade on Thursday evening
- Pageants, sporting events, craft shows and more

roll their floats down Marion's main streets to the cheers of thousands of eager people.

Throughout the three-day weekend, there will be sporting events, music, craft booths, contests and more—all in the name of popcorn, the popcorn industry and Marion.

Those who have been with the festival for a long time will note how there is something for everyone along the streets—from games and rides for the kids to a collection of activities for senior citizens. Festival staff members say they make an effort to entertain all age groups over the three-day event. A group of dedicated volunteers has been in charge of the event for the last thirty-four years and will continue to make sure each year is successful.

The festival came into Marion at a time when manufacturing businesses were leaving, a time when Marion needed something good. Through the 1980s and 1990s, it saw rapid growth. It has stood the tests of time, the 2008 recession, sponsors dropping out and threats of bad weather every year. And at a time when even air at the gas station costs money, the festival remains free and open to the public.

When the festival was founded, it was with the help of one of America's leaders in popcorn production and research. The Wyandot Popcorn Company, known as Wyandot Incorporated since 1983, was an industry giant and the largest exporter of popcorn in the world. W. Hoover Brown and his wife, Ava, founded the company in 1936; when the Popcorn Festival started, the company was in the hands of their children.

A girl looks caught between being scared and being thrilled as she rides the big yellow slide. *Marion Popcorn Festival.*

A wagon from Dan-Dee Pretzel and Chip Co. rolls through the first Marion Popcorn Festival parade. *Wyandot Popcorn Museum.*

George and Warren Brown worked to grow the sales of their parents' company as the business expanded and evolved. There were two major components of the business: the raw popcorn production plant and Popped-Right Corn Co., which specialized in corn-based salty snacks (tortilla chips, cheese curls, et cetera).

George Brown kept a history of the festival and the company until his health began failing, and it is still enshrined in the Wyandot Popcorn Museum. He died in 2010, but his family's legacy still lives on in the history of the festival and in the company that was once the largest exporter of popcorn in the world.

Chapter 1

IT ALL STARTED WITH POPCORN

With our farm income depressed, and with Ava's encouragement, I decided to go into the popcorn processing business. We thought this would bolster our income and, at the same time, allow me to continue to operate the family farm. In early May 1936, I planted 100 acres of popcorn.
—W. Hoover Brown[1]

Wyandot Incorporated is an integral part of the Popcorn Festival story, as the company helped fuel the idea of having a popcorn-related festival. From small beginnings, it grew to become the largest exporter of popcorn in the world. Today, the company employs about four hundred people.[2]

Presidential Ties

Popcorn today is a great snack for movies, watching TV or just when you need something to munch on. And it's a pretty cheap snack to get, even at a movie theater or a professional sports game. Perhaps this is why the Wyandot Popcorn Company enjoyed so much success during the Great Depression era—people just couldn't afford much else.

The Wyandot Popcorn Company began in Wyandot County, Marion County's neighbor, in 1936. It grew during the Depression years and

A portrait of W. Hoover Brown. *Brown family.*

beyond, according to the company website, as popcorn became a favorite cheap snack for people.

Its founders, W. Hoover Brown and Ava (King) Brown, dated for five years before they were married. "It was 'love at first sight,'" George wrote in his 1979 memoir. "Within a few weeks, Ava was a very special girl to me."

They lived together at the King mansion in Marion after they were married—"the biggest event of 1923, as far as Ava and I were concerned," George Brown wrote. He, as a farmer, understood the practicality of living with his wife's family and saving money.

Right across the street was the home of Warren G. Harding, a close family friend. Harding was in the White House by the time they were married, but

George recalls going to watch Harding campaign on his front porch while he and Ava were still dating.

The King family was very wealthy. Ava's father was a founder of Marion Power Shovel, an equipment-manufacturing company whose machines helped build the Panama Canal and transport NASA space shuttles to their launch pads.

Just before the two were married, Ava and her mother met the Hardings in Washington for dinner. The president and the first lady sent six dozen white roses for their wedding. And several months later, when the president died, the Kings hosted several industry leaders at their Marion home.

Henry Ford, Thomas Edison and Harvey Firestone all stayed at the Kings' for Harding's funeral. In his memoir, W. Hoover recalls an inspirational chat with Ford about farming and soybeans that he carried with him for years.

One Hundred Acres

In 1936, with farm income depressed, W. Hoover and Ava began a new adventure. The price of hogs, lambs, wheat, corn and hay all dipped.

"We thought this would bolster our income and at the same time allow me to continue to operate the family farm," Brown wrote in his memoir.

They began their business with one hundred acres of popcorn and several pieces of equipment in the old brick schoolhouse where W. Hoover spent some formative years. He and Ava invested $750, which a close friend matched, to form the Wyandot Popcorn Company.

The first crop of popcorn was processed that fall. Brown writes that it had an expansion ratio of thirty to one, whereas other companies were producing kernels with a twenty-three-to-one ratio.

The company stayed in that little schoolhouse for eight years, and husband and wife shared ownership up until it became a corporation in 1946.

"Ava was an ardent supporter of the company and truly a helpmate," W. Hoover wrote in his memoir. The Browns built a new processing plant next door.

In 1948, Wyandot expanded again. The Browns built a new facility for ready-to-eat popcorn in Marion called the Popped-Right Corn Company. Popped-Right had begun selling caramel corn by the 1950s. W. Hoover Brown turned to his friend Bert Shirk, who had years of experience in caramel corn production for his local confectionery business, Shirk's Candy.

Ava Brown named this new recipe "Golden Crisp Caramel Corn." Shirk's Candy is still a well-known name in Marion.[3]

This Wyandot subsidiary took on a major player in the 1960s. The Frito Company merged with H.W. Lay, Incorporated, and created the household name Frito-Lay. Warren Brown, the youngest of W. Hoover and Ava's sons, approached smaller chip companies and asked if Popped-Right could manufacture new lines of salty snacks under each company's brand.

With this growth, the companies needed more room. In 1964, Wyandot Popcorn and Popped-Right built new corporate offices in Marion. Though the raw popcorn–processing plant stayed in Wyandot County, the ready-to-eat corn and salty snacks came out of the new Wyandot Avenue facility.[4]

Worldwide

Wyandot began shipping raw popcorn overseas in the 1970s. Consumer demand for the snack grew both domestically and abroad, so Wyandot had a variety of products ready to ship around the globe, marketed as Pow-Wow Popcorn, Wyandot Indian Popcorn and Cowboy Popcorn, among

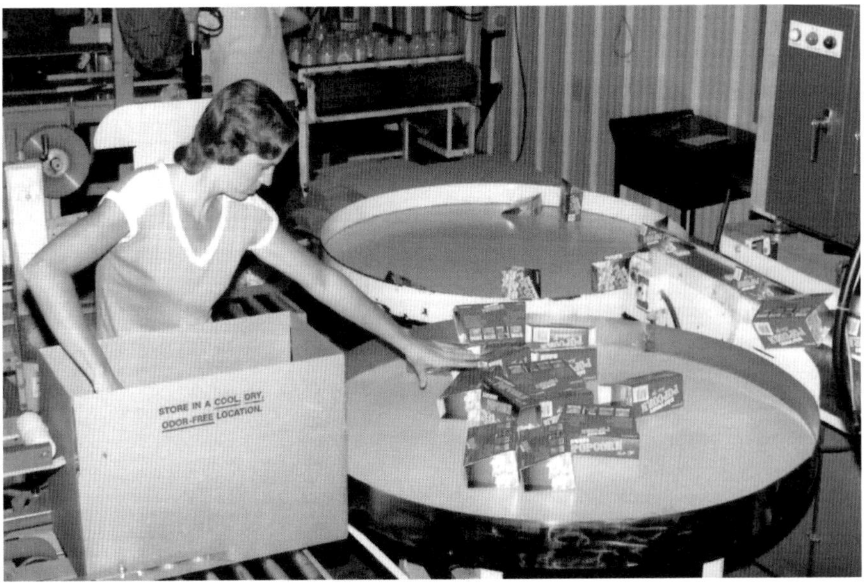

A worker in the 1980s packages popcorn boxes at the Wyandot Popcorn Factory. *Wyandot Popcorn Museum.*

others. Products went to Australia, Japan, Taiwan, Central America, South America, Africa, Europe and the Middle East.

In addition to the traditional fifty- and one-hundred-pound bags sold to theaters and stadiums, the company also offered raw popcorn in cans, jars and microwave packages. From 1974 to 1980, Wyandot's raw popcorn sales doubled from twenty-five to fifty million pounds annually.

Around the time of the Marion Popcorn Festival, Wyandot was the world's leading exporter of popcorn. With sales in seventy-five countries,

Pow-Wow Popcorn was one of Wyandot's main labels. *Wyandot Popcorn Museum.*

"Super S" labels from Wyandot's international sales. *Wyandot Popcorn Museum.*

the central Ohio company accounted for about 25 percent of total global popcorn sales.

George Brown concentrated on growing Wyandot's international sales of raw popcorn, and Warren worked to expand Popped-Right's snack sales.

Brooks Brown remembered that in the 1980s, the company was "always" working on varieties of popcorn and researching both pop speed and the stability of the popped corn. Movie theater popcorn and the popcorn used for caramel corn are two different types; caramel corn needs to be much sturdier, he says.

So "Super X" kernels were known for their expansion ratio. "Super C" were known for their mushroom-style shape and sturdy bodies. Coating popcorn in caramel, especially in mass amounts, can definitely cause breaks in the fragile food.

"They would tend to ball more," Brown said. "They were intended for a different purpose. You could coat it without breaking off all the little wings."

At the time, Brown said, most kernels would expand at a ratio of forty to one. He said some of Wyandot's kernels had a fifty-to-one expansion ratio.

"At that point, we were going to a number of theater chains and saying, 'Hey, with this corn you can fill this many more boxes of popcorn with our customers, and therefore you'll make hundreds of dollars more per fifty-pound bag,'" he said. Some movie theaters bought into the idea, while others stuck to what they knew.

Super M (manufacturing) was a third hybrid and was preferred by automated manufacturing plants because of its large kernel that resisted crumbling.

As popcorn research was expanding, so were salty snack offerings. By 1980, Popped-Right was offering butter- and cheese-flavored popcorn, caramel corn, extruded cheese puffs, crunchy cheese puffs, corn chips and plain and nacho-flavored tortilla chips. The company bought a facility in

Microwaveable popcorn boxes roll off of the assembly line at the Wyandot Popcorn Company. *Wyandot Popcorn Museum.*

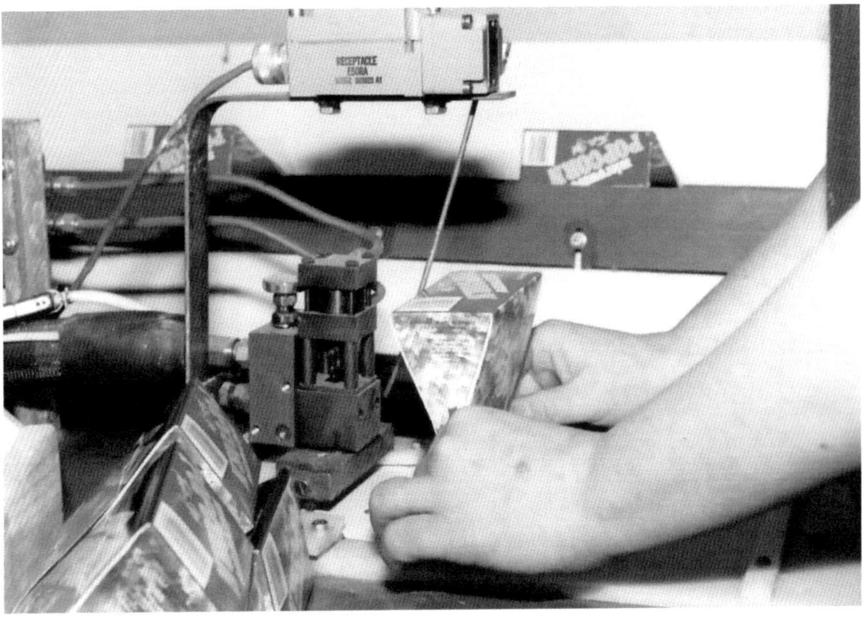

Careful hands fold up a microwavable popcorn box at the Wyandot Popcorn Factory. *Wyandot Popcorn Museum.*

Jeffersonville, Indiana, to continue growth and take a foray into the potato chip industry.

In 1983, the Popped-Right name was discontinued, but both the raw popcorn processing and salty-snack manufacturing continued under the name Wyandot, Incorporated.

And the name became well known. As grocery chains began to carry "store brands" of a wide variety of products in the 1980s, Wyandot quickly became the quality manufacturer of choice throughout the country. Soon, Wyandot had significant sales to "private label" grocers across North America. Even actor and philanthropist Paul Newman, a friend of George Brown's, called on the company to produce some of his products.[5]

The Change

In 1989, Wyandot sold its raw popcorn–processing operation. Brooks Brown said that sales were up and down and that popcorn was "too much of a commodity."

"It could be tough depending on the market conditions," he said. "The snack side of the business kind of carried it in those years. We were growing more rapidly on the snack side."

The company that bought the raw processing section of the company went under, and ConAgra Foods took over the production. ConAgra, which is known for brands such as Orville Redenbacher's, Jif and Healthy Choice, has a major plant in Marion that will shut its doors later in 2014.

On November 1, 1996, Wyandot suffered a fire at its Marion manufacturing facility. Wyandot's Jeffersonville, Indiana teammates ran their facility around the clock for the eight months it took for the Marion plant to recover. As many as sixteen different snack manufacturers, many of them competitors, partnered with Wyandot to help fill customer orders. The company did not lose a single customer after the fire.[6]

In 2001, Wyandot's sales exceeded the $100 million mark for the first time. By 2006, the company had sold its Jeffersonville, Indiana manufacturing facility (used for potato chip processing) in order to concentrate its efforts on corn-based snacks.

Now, Brooks Brown is Wyandot's national sales manager. The company makes corn-based snacks for some of the largest restaurant and grocery chains around. And though the only popcorn coming out of the facility today is caramel and kettle corn, he says people still remember the company for its early staples.

"A lot of people still call us Wyandot Popcorn," he said.

Wyandot's clientele is mostly private, but Brown says they are very busy making tortilla chips, corn chips, flat crisps, cereal-based snacks, extruded snacks (also known as "cheese puffs" to the laypeople) and all the flavor combinations in between. The company's clientele have included Frito-Lay, Proctor & Gamble, Kraft Foods, Aldi, McDonald's, Wendy's and Bob Evans.

"We're so busy," he said. "We're running three shifts a day, almost seven days a week."

The Museum

The current Wyandot Popcorn Museum hosts the world's largest collection of popcorn poppers and peanut roasters and sits right in downtown Marion with the Marion Historical Society.

A popcorn/peanut wagon parked by the Harding Memorial. *Wyandot Popcorn Museum.*

Gleaming machines, the largest collection of restored antiques in the world, sit under a striped tent and transport visitors back to the early to mid-1900s. Some of the poppers are even from the late 1800s. It's easy to imagine someone pushing a popcorn wagon down the street at the Ohio State Fair and selling popcorn to eager young kids or making some money in the middle of a busy park as families look for something to snack on.

The museum started in the early 1970s and '80s. George Brown, son of Wyandot Popcorn founders Ava and W. Hoover Brown, was the key player in the museum's creation. Today, there is a large wedding cake–style display in the center of the museum about Wyandot and the Brown family.

At the time of the first festival, George was in the process of researching the history of popcorn. His son, Brooks, said the collection of antiques spawned from this project.

"He always wanted to write the history of popcorn," Brooks said. "He gathered a ton of information over the years…he never officially wrote [a book], but they started collecting the antiques as a result and created this amazing museum."

The museum's original spot was in an old schoolhouse where W. Hoover Brown attended elementary school. But as the collection grew, this small space was not enough. The museum moved to the Wyandot Popcorn Company and to Marion's Southland Mall.

About 1988, some of the machines moved around. Three antique poppers, including a 1915 Kingery walk-in wagon, a 1948 Air-Popt automatic vendor and a 1912 Cretors No. 1 steam wagon, went to the Center of Science & Industry (COSI) in Columbus. One antique went to the Snack Food Association in Alexandria, Virginia. Two antiques went to Paul Newman's office in Westport, Connecticut. Other local antiques were returned to their owners.

The Cretors Model TT Ford concession wagon was temporarily stored in George Brown's barn, along with a 1911 Dunbar wagon formerly owned by Paul Newman. The rest of the antiques went to Michael and Linda Perry's bed-and-breakfast on South State Street in Marion. Most of the first floor of this home was used to display the various antiques.

The collection settled at the old U.S. Post Office in 1989 and still stands there today.

Popcorn Popper History

Charles Cretors first showed off a steam-powered peanut roaster and popcorn popper outside his confectionary shop in Chicago, but it wasn't until the 1893 Midway of Chicago's Columbian Exposition that he drew in big crowds with the smell of buttered popcorn and a clown mascot called the Toasty Roasty Man. His machine could roast twelve pounds of peanuts and twenty pounds of coffee, pop corn and bake chestnuts all at the same time. People were fascinated.

He introduced a horse-drawn popcorn wagon in 1900 and created the first popcorn machine with an electric motor later that decade. Competition began emerging after 1910, and the Wyandot Popcorn Museum features several other companies' poppers.

C. Cretors and Co. still produces large concession poppers, gourmet retail equipment, hot dog equipment and ice/food shavers.

The Wyandot Popcorn Museum currently hosts Advance, Air-Popt, Bartholomew, Burch, Cretors, Dunbar, Emerson Brothers, Excel, Holcomb & Hoke, Kingery, Long, Long-Eakin, Manley, Olsen, Star and Stutsman antiques.[7]

George Brown behind the wheel of his beloved popcorn wagon, which he drove every year in the parade. *Wyandot Popcorn Museum.*

The museum display currently includes Advance, Air-Popt, Bartholomew, Burch, Cretors, Dunbar, Emerson Brothers, Excel, Holcomb & Hoke, Kingery, Long, Long-Eakin, Manley, Olsen, Star and Stutsman antiques, according to its website.[8]

In one corner of the museum, rows of red binders hold years of popcorn history. George Brown compiled information on Wyandot, on popcorn poppers, on the popcorn industry and on Marion's own Popcorn Festival before his death in 2010.

Brooks recalled how his father would get the 1927 Cretors Model TT popcorn wagon out of the museum every year, put on a popcorn sweatshirt and join the parade.

"It was a huge deal to get out of the museum; you had to hoist it down the ramp, and sometimes it wouldn't start," he said. "We'd stall in the middle of the parade."

But his dad loved the parade, so he would drive the wagon every year wearing his popcorn sweatshirt, sweating the whole time.

"That was his joy," Brooks said. "It'd almost bring tears to his eyes to drive down that parade route and wave to his friends in the community. He loved it, he absolutely loved it."

ConAgra

Another major popcorn player in the Marion area is ConAgra Foods, which is headquartered in Omaha.

When Wyandot Incorporated sold its popcorn division in 1989, it went to investors in Chicago. Vogel Popcorn, a division of Golden Valley, bought it from the bank a year later. ConAgra now owns Golden Valley, and the company had previously purchased Orville Redenbacher's Gourmet Popping Corn in the 1970s.[9]

For an interview George Brown did with Orville Redenbacher in 1981, see Appendix A.

ConAgra's Marion plant, which is scheduled to close in the fall of 2014, produces popcorn under the Orville Redenbacher name. It previously produced Jiffy Pop and Act II brands, as well.[10] The company is the Popcorn Festival's largest donor as of 2014.

Dan Skinner, public relations/social media manager for ConAgra, said the Marion plant has been in operation since 1945 and has produced food under the ConAgra name since 1991. He said the Marion team is very active in the community.

"Every year, we have sponsored the parade that kicks off the Thursday opening night of the festival," he said. "Of course, this celebration of popcorn heritage and history is a source of pride for the members of the Marion plant team.

"The Marion plant supports a number of other community efforts, including making donations to local food pantries and local high school athletic teams who sell popcorn at their concession stands," he added. "The plant has also provided popcorn for local events managed by the Red Cross."

Chapter 2

MARION

The city of Marion is about fifty miles north of Ohio's capital, Columbus. And the county is definitely full of Ohio State University fans, even if it would take many residents over an hour to get down to the stadium.

The town and county were founded in the early 1800s. As of 2010, there were 36,837 residents within the city limits and a total of 66,501 in the county.

At the time the Popcorn Festival was founded, Marion was known as an industrial hub, though business was beginning to decline. Today, Marion's largest employer is Whirlpool Corp., the largest dryer manufacturer in the world. Other major industrial employers include Silver Line Windows and Doors (an Andersen Company), Wyandot Incorporated, Nucor Steel Marion Incorporated and General Mills. A large number of people in the county still farm, and people driving into the county from a state route or U.S. highway will probably pass fields on their way. Approximately 80 percent of Marion County's land area is devoted to farming, with corn, soybeans, hogs and dairy cattle as the principal products.

There are higher education opportunities at the Ohio State University–Marion campus, Marion Technical College and Tri-Rivers Career Center, a hub for training in robotics. Marion City Schools and four surrounding county school districts provide K-12 education.[11]

Among one of the many sporting events at the festival is corn hole—a Midwest tradition! *Marion Popcorn Festival.*

A boy reaches out to feed a kangaroo at the 2010 festival. *Marion Popcorn Festival.*

Marion History

Marion County was inhabited by Delaware and Wyandot tribes before white settlers came in.

The first permanent white settlers came into what is now Waldo Township, in southern Marion County, in 1806, with subsequent settlements coming in 1814 and 1815.

Marion County became its own entity, separate from its southern neighbor Delaware County, in December 1823. In the years to come, the county would absorb land from and lose land to neighboring counties (Crawford, Wyandot, Morrow, Union and Delaware).

The town and county were named for famed Revolutionary War general Francis Marion.

The town of Marion was founded in 1822 and named the county seat soon after.

The first railroad in the county was the Bellefontaine and Indiana Railroad.

At the turn of the twentieth century, Marion was growing in part due to its renovated railroads and its manufacturing.

Before its manufacturing days, however, it was not known for industry. J.W. Jacoby writes, "In the earlier days there were no manufacturing establishment[s] of importance. In 1846 there was one sawmill and one fulling, oil and carding mill."[12]

Its Place in History

As previously mentioned, Marion is probably best known for being the hometown and burial site of Warren G. Harding, twenty-ninth president of the United States. Harding, though known for the scandals that hung over his short term in office, was also known for his affability and his strong foreign policy.

Harding owned Marion's newspaper, the *Marion Daily Star*, which still prints daily as the *Marion Star*. He ran much of his presidential campaign on his front porch, often drawing huge crowds to Marion. W. Hoover Brown and Ava King Brown would often watch his front porch speeches while they were dating.

The Harding Home is a short distance from downtown and would make an easy trip for any curious Popcorn Festival attendees. The home, built between 1890 and 1891,[13] contains many of the Hardings' personal belongings and memories of before the family moved to Washington, D.C. Clothes, musical instruments, golf clubs, pipes and even the Hardings' old waffle iron are in the comfortable home.

Though there are no anecdotes to be found about Harding and popcorn (the snack was not popular until after his death), he might have enjoyed the Marion Popcorn Festival if any of the vendors carried waffles. The president's wisdom on breakfast food is etched on a plaque in his kitchen: "You eat the first fourteen waffles without syrup, but with lots of butter. Then you put syrup on the next nine, and the last half-dozen you eat simply swimming in syrup. Eaten that way, waffles never hurt anybody."

His tomb, a magnificent structure cast in marble, is also very close to downtown. His wife, Florence, is also buried at the site.

Several other notable people are from Marion, including industrialist Edward Huber, former United States treasurer Mary Ellen Withrow,

People mill around the street at the 1995 Marion Popcorn Festival. *Marion Popcorn Festival.*

American Civil Liberties Union founder Norman Thomas and former Major League Baseball umpire Larry Barnett.

As history goes, there are several other museums in the county besides the Harding Home and Museum and the Wyandot Popcorn Museum. Heritage Hall, where the Popcorn Museum is stationed, contains a restored schoolhouse and myriad artifacts, including some from Harding's time. The Huber Machinery Museum holds a history of what eventually became Marion Power Shovel. Edward Huber is credited for revolutionizing the farming industry with his revolving hay rake and other inventions. Marion Union Station is a crossroads for two modern railroad companies and contains railroad memorabilia from Marion's history with the industry. Civil War–era artifacts are housed in the Stengel True Museum, and the Buckeye Telephone Museum is the spot to check out a collection of telephones throughout the years.

Downtown Marion, where the Popcorn Festival takes place, hosts a number of independently owned stores and restaurants. Visitors for the festival or just for fun can find other historical sites, parks, shops and restaurants in the city and county of Marion.

Chapter 3

A KERNEL OF AN IDEA

At the time of the first festival, Marion was in a bit of an economic downturn.

Several major employers headed out of town in the 1970s and early 1980s, and a few railroad lines shut down. For a working-class county, this was a tough blow. Longtime Marion residents recall the mentality at the time: "last one out, turn out the lights."

Mike Nicolosi owned a restaurant at the time called the Scotch and Sirloin and said he would often throw around ideas with his friends Mark Schwartzkopf and Pat Regules over a beer or two. One of the main things they would talk about was how to bring excitement to the community. They wanted something exciting and something that would last. Previous efforts had failed, and they wanted something good.

"Of course, we were thinking something small," Regules laughed as he recalled the early planning stages.

Both Nicolosi and Schwartzkopf were in the food industry. Their first idea was an international food festival, Nicolosi said. But they decided rural Marion might not be the best place for that because there isn't a large ethnic population in town. Nearby towns had the Bratwurst Festival and the Pumpkin Festival, but Marion isn't known for those foods. So, they thought: what was their town known for other than Warren G. Harding and Edward Huber?

At the time, Wyandot Incorporated was the largest exporter of popcorn in the world. So the three men and some of their friends sat down with the Brown family to talk about creating a popcorn festival.

They spent the next year planning with about twenty other people in the community—communications experts, ad agents and other local leaders. The goal they had in mind was to promote Marion and provide free name entertainment to the public. They decided to have the festival on the first weekend after Labor Day, when the weather is still warm but isn't oppressively hot like July or August.

Nicolosi said a key goal for the founders was to give festival-goers a good show.

"The theme was that we were going to have the Popcorn Festival…along with that, we were going to have name entertainment free to the public. That was our main goal," he said.

More than thirty years down the road, that hasn't changed.

"This whole thing has changed its complexion a little bit, but it still focuses on that free entertainment," Nicolosi said.

Norma Castanien served as the first secretary-treasurer. She recalls Schwartzkopf coming up to her one night and asking her to take part in his new venture. She couldn't say no.

"They were sitting around the bar one night talking…and a bunch of us girls were over in another corner. Mark came up to me, he said, 'How'd you like to be secretary-treasurer of a new organization?' and I said 'Oh sure, Mark, anything you want.'"

A few meetings later and the group was planning the inaugural Popcorn Festival.

"We wanted to get Marion back on the map," Castanien remembers. "That's really how it started."

Mayor Ron Malone's administration was on board, as well. It is key, Nicolosi said, to have the support of the local government (especially when asking to shut down streets for a festival).

Schwartzkopf, who died recently, was one of the driving forces behind the festival. He, Nicolosi, Castanien and Richard "Dick" Rees are the names listed on the official registration with the Ohio secretary of state.

The festival founders established a board of trustees and an executive board, consisting of a president, first and second vice-president, a secretary-treasurer and a fifth appointed officer. While the president makes most of the business decisions, he or she appoints a director to oversee most of the festival committee chairs.

Schwartzkopf was the first president, and Regules filled the first director's position when the time came.

"We were having fun," Regules said. "It was like a small family of people."

When the festival committee wrote out a charter, the members established several goals for the annual event, including:

- To further the common good and general welfare of the people of the community by promoting and sponsoring an annual summer festival in and about the streets, ways and public places in and about the city of Marion, Ohio;
- To promote the community throughout the State of Ohio and the nation;
- To contribute to the economy of the Marion area and foster civic pride and community spirit in the city of Marion, Ohio among all its citizens.

Now for the Fun Part

So the idea was sound, but none of them had ever started a festival from scratch before.

"We had *no* idea what we were doing," Nicolosi laughed. "We were just out there floundering around."

They took about a year to plan, but there was certainly a lot to do. How would they pay for it? How many vendors could they get? What would the entertainment options look like? And most importantly, how many local residents would show up?

"One thing led to another, and we decided to have some entertainment," Regules said. "It built up to quite a project, especially for that first year."

Nicolosi recalls going to the nearby Bucyrus Bratwurst Festival to get ideas and to ask concession vendors to come to Marion. He served as concession chair at first, so it was his job to get enough vendors to line the streets. He was aiming for the stars, of course, but no one had a clue if they would have guests at the festival to keep the concessionaires busy.

"I was trying to get them on board and not knowing if we were gonna have one person come through that line," Nicolosi said.

Several concessionaires have been with the festival all thirty-four years, including Schmidt's Sausage Haus of Columbus. Nicolosi remembers that the Schmidts wanted to be the only concessionaire at the festival, and they balked when he told them he was expecting to have one hundred different vendors. He said he asked the owners to just give his festival a chance, and they agreed.

Vendors line up and get ready to start the day. *Marion Popcorn Festival.*

Of course, if they *had* been the only ones, they wouldn't have been able to keep up with all the people who came to the first festival. Even so, a well-known vendor brought people by the bunches.

"People flooded that thing," he said. "They [the company] liked it so much that they've been back every year."

The first year, there were a lot of local concessionaires, as well as out-of-towners. Several local school boosters, Lions' Clubs and other nonprofits sat side by side with the big, gleaming food trucks.

Regules took charge of the beer gardens, using a mobile home he owned with his wife, Kathy, as the festival office.

A local Anheuser-Busch distributing plant helped set up beer gardens around the festival, and there was live entertainment in each little section. Nicolosi said that, in the beginning, food and drink made up most of the budget.

"That was the heart of the festival because that's where all the money was generated; concessionaires paying for space created the revenue so we could go out and get that free entertainment," he said. "We got corporate sponsors eventually."

The city volunteered emergency protection, the water company helped clean the streets and supplied vendors and the electric company brought cable. But there wasn't enough cable to power the amusement rides *and* the vendors, so a few people went down to Columbus to ask desperately for more wiring.

"I'll never forget going down to the Columbus State Fair...and this was like three or four days before our festival," Nicolosi said. "And we were down there *begging* for cable, and finally we got to the right people; they let us have this cable."

He said the festival founders used all kinds of media to advertise, including print, radio and Columbus-area television stations. George and Janice Scantlands, a local couple who owned their own radio station, helped get the word out over the airwaves.

Put to the Test

The first year was an absolute success. A combination of hard work, good advertising and local enthusiasm brought crowds downtown—locals, out-of-towners and even folks from other states.

"Every little piece brought people to town," Nicolosi remembered. "Along with Marion, Ohio, the county hasn't changed much. It was still about sixty to seventy thousand people."

The Dan-Dee Pretzel and Chip Co. wagon appeared in the first-ever Popcorn Festival. *Marion Popcorn Festival.*

People on a tour of the Wyandot Popcorn Company in 1981. *Wyandot Popcorn.*

A worker at the Wyandot Popcorn Museum. *Wyandot Popcorn Museum.*

As it has every year, the festival began with a parade.

"That was an amazing thing for us to stand back and watch the whole thing develop—and people love a parade," Nicolosi said. "So they came down in droves just to watch."

There was also a tour of the Wyandot facilities.

Castanien said the founders were amazed at how many people showed up.

"We didn't know what was going to happen," said Castanien, also a past president of the festival. "We kept saying, 'Why'd they all come?'"

A photo published in the *Marion Star* shows the extent of the parade's first audience. *Marion Popcorn Festival.*

She recalls standing with a friend on the midway and being shocked at the number of people there.

The Lettermen, Henny Youngman and Ray Stevens played the very first Popcorn Festival. Nicolosi recalled the sense of pride and joy he felt as he and Mark Schwartzkopf stood at the Lettermen show with their wives.

"Tears are just running down our eyes as we're watching the Lettermen, and we turn around and we look and see this sea of people. There had to be forty to fifty thousand people sitting in the back. It was amazing."

Regules remembers that he had to pay the first artists with cash—so he and his wife, Kathy, sat in the little office and counted all the money coming in from the beer gardens.

"It was so thrilling, really, that it was a success," he said. "We were scrambling. We weren't totally prepared for that kind of an activity, but we got through it. It gave us a lot of confidence that we could make something even more."

It was quite a feat for a group of friends—or drinking buddies, as Regules would say.

An estimated 50,000 people watched the first parade, and about 200,000 were at the inaugural event. The planning committee couldn't believe it.

People work on a float ahead of the first Marion Popcorn Festival. *Wyandot Popcorn Museum.*

"We were just flabbergasted. We knew it was gonna be a nice festival, but we had no idea of how many people were gonna be at this thing," Nicolosi said.

Even an event that was hastily thrown together had a good turnout. Castanien said the first Popcorn Queen pageant was a "last-minute thing," but twenty-seven women showed up to vie for the crown.

The first festival drew about 200,000 people, and the executive board went into immediate planning mode soon after. It brought in $58,679.99 and spent $58,231.03—a small profit of $448.96.

"I don't think any of us saw the big picture at the time," Nicolosi reflected. "We were just having a good time. It was just fun putting it together. The first few years of anything is always the best time."

Chapter 4

MAINTAINING EXCELLENCE

Popcorn Festival veterans say the event would not have lasted this long without the help of the volunteers, committee members, sponsors, downtown businesses and community folks along the way. Thousands of dollars flow in and out of the city every year for the festival.

A group gathers at Wyandot. *Wyandot Popcorn Museum.*

A girl participates in the 2012 Kiddie Tractor Pull. *Marion Popcorn Festival.*

Through the years, though events and traditions have changed, the commitment of volunteers and committee members has fueled the annual celebration.

Several sponsors have come and gone over the years. Current major contributors include ConAgra, Marion General Hospital, Ohio Health, McDonald's, Thiel's Wheels, Huntington Bank, Wyandot Incorporated and Silver Line Windows and Doors.

During the 1980s and 1990s, the festival cemented itself as one of the premier events in the Midwest, calling up well-known entertainers and celebrities for the main stage and for the parade route.

"We were having fun," Pat Regules said. "It was like a small family."

The 1980s: Building a New Tradition

In 1982, the Wyandot Museum and Factory Outlet Store opened for tours. "Jungle" Jack Hanna and his wife, Kathy, came up from the Columbus Zoo to entertain the children. Helen Reddy, Lee Greenwood and The Spinners took the stage as headline performers.

Cyclists make their way through Marion for the 2009 Popcorn 100. *Marion Popcorn Festival.*

By 1983, the Popcorn Festival was the second-largest festival in Ohio. The Righteous Brothers and the Four Tops played on Friday night, and T.G. Sheppard was Saturday's main stage player. This year was the first that the festival held sporting events: the Popcorn 100 bicycle tour, a "run for fun," the Mixed Kernels Tennis Open, the Shoot-Out Softball Tournament and a long drive contest.

Legendary Ohio State University football coach Woody Hayes was grand marshal of the ever-growing Popcorn Parade in 1984. On the main stage were the Pointer Sisters, Louise Mandrell, The Guess Who and Atlanta. Actor Paul Newman chose Wyandot to produce his "Newman's Own Old Style Picture Show Popcorn" in this year. Also, festival-goers got to see quite a sight: a fourteen-foot, 3,020-pound popcorn ball constructed as a fundraiser for the Arthritis Foundation.

In its fifth year, the festival was accepted into the Ohio Festivals Association. This was the first year that the annual pageants became scholarship competitions for the young women involved. The Charlie Daniels Band and the Commodores were the big names on stage. The year 1985 was the first for the "Tri Ear-Thalon," a sticky and complex athletic event. Several teams participated in a series of four contests: a bed race, a corn-husking relay, a wheelbarrow race and a tug-of-war over caramel corn.

By 1986, there were an estimated one thousand volunteers helping make the festival a success. And the Popcorn Festival Scholarship Pageant expanded to include a total of seven counties. Tanya Tucker and Cheap Trick were in town to perform.

In 1987, the festival welcomed Michael McDonald, the Gatlin Brothers and the Coasters. An estimated sixty thousand people watched the parade this year. By 1987, major sponsors such as grocery giant Kroger were helping the festival continue to provide entertainment year after year.

In 1988, Gloria Estefan, Eddie Rabbit and Steve Somerlot were the main headliners. The festival continued its tradition of sporting events, with the Popcorn 100 and Tri Ear-Thalon among the fun challenges.

The year 1989 featured a Pop Shot Photo Contest and a Popcorn Bowl sponsored by Marion Midget Football. There were an estimated 250 entries and 3,000 marchers in the parade. REO Speedwagon fans packed the streets for the rock band's show; B.J. Thomas, the McCarters and JoAnn Castle also entertained the crowds.[14]

Year Ten

By 1990, the tenth anniversary, hundreds of thousands of people were showing up on the streets of Marion. The parade had reached three hundred entries, and the festival had two big names prepared to entertain: Smokey Robinson followed by Joan Jett and the Blackhearts the next evening.

Among the festivities were the Popcorn 100 cycling tour, the Tri Ear-Thalon contest, the parade and pageants and a 5K road race.

Sam Birnbaum, president of the Popcorn Board in 1990, said he was amazed at the festival's success.

"Once people learn that the first festival was put together in just a few months and that organizers started from scratch with no money, it's amazing to think that the festival has grown to one of the largest events in Ohio," he was quoted as saying in the 1990 souvenir program.

"We thought the crowd probably came out because of the free entertainment, so that's why we put so much emphasis on the entertainment," he continued. "The more money the festival makes, the more money

A local artist works on a piece at the festival. *Marion Popcorn Festival.*

available to bring in national entertainment, which attracts more people, who spend more money, which can fund bigger stars."

He reflected that the parade has gotten bigger and better every year.

"What's worthwhile is watching kids' faces as the parade passes by, listening as people sing along or cheer for their favorite entertainers and watching the people eat the food and stroll along the grounds having a good time," he said. "That's why the festival is worthwhile, I believe. We just want to make sure that people who come have fun and go home with a good feeling about our town."[15]

The festival spent an estimated $120,000 in the Marion community in 1988 and 1989.[16]

The 1990s: Continued Growth

The festival was named one of the American Bus Association's "Top 100 Events in North America" in 1992, the same year George Jones and Jan and Dean took the stage. David Lee Roth, Willie Nelson, Kansas, Aaron Tippin, Huey Lewis and the News, Aaron Neville and others were main stage entertainers in the 1990s. Tom Jones was too ill to play the main stage in 1998, but his band came to entertain the crowd.

An artist works the crowd at the festival. *Marion Popcorn Festival.*

A collection of royalty from the 1991 festival. *Marion Popcorn Festival.*

Crowds gather on the street at the 1995 festival. *Marion Popcorn Festival.*

There was a slight layout change in 1993. The parade route and festival map have remained mostly the same since then. Local and national names served as marshals in this decade of popcorn parading.

The Kroger Co. sponsored a float in the 1991 parade. *Marion Popcorn Festival.*

Many of the same events recurred year after year, including the Popcorn 100 bike tour, 5K run, craft booths and tennis tournament. The festival was recognized by the Ohio State Auditor's office in 1997 for its contribution to Ohio tourism.[17]

The festival reached attendance heights in the 1990s as well. Marion resident Elizabeth Foos said she remembers Michael McDonald and Huey Lewis's shows and that she would often take her son Kyle to the festival when he was young. She said she enjoyed some of the early mornings before it got too crowded—there was still plenty to see and do.

"When I worked downtown, I much enjoyed walking out the doors at lunchtime and enjoying the wonderful variety of cuisine and aromas, crowd free," she said. "My son, when he was young, and I would come to the festival early on Saturday, as I much enjoyed browsing the craft tents, meeting the artisans and merchants. Also, Kyle enjoyed the kiddie rides."

Year Twenty

The festival celebrated its twentieth anniversary in the new millennium. Rock band Styx and country singer Pam Tillis were the main entertainers during "20 Years of Poppin' Good Times."

By 2000, it had become the largest popcorn-themed festival in the world. Steve Somerlot, president at the time, remarked on how amazed he was that the festival had lasted so long.

"And when you stop and think about the thousands of visitors, the thousands of dollars spent and the thousands of hours put in by our volunteers, it's no wonder we continue to be one of the premier events in Ohio and the country," he was quoted as saying in a twentieth-anniversary souvenir magazine.

Nicolosi, Castanien and Hendrix also remarked on its successes.

Pop P. Corn, the festival mascot, waves to the crowd in 2010. *Marion Popcorn Festival.*

Clowns hanging out at the 1995 festival. *Wyandot Popcorn Museum.*

"You hear stories related of people who come back to Marion for the festival because they see so many old friends," Castanien said. "Others who live right here in town run into old schoolmates they haven't seen in years. Then there are the casual acquaintances who only see each other once a year—on the streets of downtown Marion in early September!"

A new mascot, Pop P. Corn, was welcomed in 2000. At six feet tall, this smiling ear of corn is still visible at annual fests. Pop P. replaced three smaller mascots named Kernel, Carmella and Poppy.[18]

A New Millennium: Spreading the Word

Since 2000, the festival has been featured in a number of magazines, newspapers, TV shows, online articles and books. The Travel Channel filmed part of an episode for *Taste of America with Mark DeCarlo* in Marion in 2004. The festival was featured on the Food Network as well, in the "All-American Festivals" series. The *Columbus Dispatch*, *Columbus Alive!*, the *Marion Star* and other area publications have featured the festival in the past.

A trio of festival-goers laughs while riding the Scrambler. *Marion Popcorn Festival.*

A man pilots his John Deere down the street for the Popcorn Festival parade. *Marion Popcorn Festival.*

Country star Blake Shelton performs at the 2007 festival. *Marion Popcorn Festival.*

Boyz II Men performed at the 2012 Marion Popcorn Festival. *Marion Popcorn Festival.*

Author Andrew F. Smith mentions the festival several times in *Popped Culture: A Social History of Popcorn in America*, and the festival is also mentioned in *Popcorn Cleans Up* by Muhammad Fayed. A book called *Yuzi's False Alarm*, part of the Secret Keeper Girl series, takes place in Marion. Its titular character has to wear a popcorn mascot costume at the behest of her mother during the Popcorn Festival.

Beyond all the press, of course, the festival continues to provide top entertainment. Recent performers include Grace Potter and the Nocturnals, Survivor, Foreigner, Trick Pony, Blake Shelton, the Village People and Boyz II Men.[19]

Chapter 5

ENTERTAINING THE MASSES

Without a doubt, one of the festival's hallmarks is the free main stage entertainment. People pour into the area around the stage and stand out in the street to get a glimpse of whatever recording artist is playing the show. Beer is flowing, the sun is setting and tickets didn't cost most people anything unless they paid extra to sit close to the stage.

Table I

Popcorn Artists Throughout the Years

1981 Ray Stevens The Lettermen Henny Youngman	**1982** Helen Reddy Lee Greenwood The Spinners Art Mooney (Guy Lombardo's Royal Canadian Band) (Palace Theatre)	**1983** The Four Tops The Righteous Brothers T.G. Shepherd
1984 Louise Mandrell Atlanta The Pointer Sisters The Guess Who	**1985** Charlie Daniels The Commodores Phil Dirt and the Dozers	**1986** Tanya Tucker Cheap Trick Restless Heart

1987 Michael McDonald Larry Gatlin and the Gatlin Brothers The Coasters The Vogues (Palace Theatre)	**1988** Gloria Estefan and the Miami Sound Machine Eddie Rabbitt The Shirelles The Girls Next Door	**1989** REO Speedwagon B.J. Thomas The McCarters JoAnn Castle (Palace Theatre)
1990 The Four Freshman Smokey Robinson Joan Jett and the Blackhearts	**1991** The Statler Brothers Eddie Money U.S. Air Force Band Bill Pinkey and the Original Drifters (Palace Theatre)	**1992** The Oakridge Boys George Jones Jan and Dean Ralna English (Palace Theatre)
1993 The Neville Brothers Waylon Jennings Three Dog Night Myron Floren (Palace Theatre)	**1994** Kathy Mattea David Lee Roth Fabulous Flashbacks The Four Lads (Palace Theatre)	**1995** Lorrie Morgan Loverboy (Foreigner cancelled) Frankie Yankovic (main stage and Palace Theatre)
1996 Willie Nelson Firehouse and Romantics (Night Ranger cancelled) 1964 (a tribute to the Beatles) Vaudvillities (Palace Theatre)	**1997** Aaron Tippin Kansas Mike Albert (Memories of Elvis) The Fox Brothers (Palace Theatre)	**1998** Clay Walker Tom Jones (cancelled, his band performed) The Vogues
1999 Joey Dee and the Starliters Huey Lewis and the News Sammy Kershaw The Ragtime Strutters (Palace)	**2000** Bill Sims Styx Pam Tillis Richens Timms Irish Dance Troupe (Palace)	**2001** Kool and the Gang Joe Diffie The Platters (main stage and Palace)

2002 The Van-Dells 38 Special Marty Stuart	**2003** Neal McCoy Steppenwolf Ricci Martin	**2004** Rick Brunetto Big Band The Danger Brothers Honky Tonk Tailgate Party BTO
2005 Parrot Head Band Foreigner Mark Chesnutt	**2006** KISS Army Mickey Thomas and Starship Trick Pony	**2007** Hells Bells Radio Pirates Blake Shelton Gin Blossoms (canceled due to weather)
2008 Draw the Line Soul Cadence Phil Vassar Molly Hatchet	**2009** Number One Bad Boys (Poison Tribute) November Rain (G-N-R Tribute) Sawyer Brown Survivor	**2010** Kentucky Headhunters Joe Nichols Blues Travelers
2011 Vicious Cycle (Lynyrd Skynyrd Tribute) Grace Potter and the Nocturnals Jason Michael Carroll	**2012** The Ultimate Journey Xperience Josh Thompson Boyz II Men Derrick & Derrick	**2013** The Village People Jo Dee Messina Wanted (Bon Jovi Tribute) Robert James McArthur (Neil Diamond Tribute)

Norma Castanien has been with the festival since its inception and now serves as chair of "Kernel Seats," a special section close to the stage at the main stage shows. She said it was important to the founders to keep the festival free at first. For one, they weren't sure how many people would pay to get in. But additionally, they wanted to provide entertainment for people from all walks of life.

"They wanted people that really don't get out to see live name entertainment; they wanted them to be able to see it," she said.

Pat Regules spent four terms as director and one as president, and he still helps coordinate the stage setup for the yearly festival.

Grace Potter and the Nocturnals played the festival in 2011. *Marion Popcorn Festival.*

His wife, Kathy, said most entertainers have been wonderful to work with. Several of them were still under the radar when they played the festival. Pat remembers country singer Lee Greenwood being virtually anonymous as he visited the festival—but a short time later, his song "God Bless the U.S.A." hit it big. Greenwood sat right in their trailer and walked around a bit, and no one knew who he was.

Kathy would often drive the performers to and from the airport. She took singer-songwriter Michael McDonald to the Marion Centre Mall when he played in 1987. There, too, hardly anyone recognized the famous singer.

"[I took him] to Radio Shack," she said. "We walked through the mall, and nobody recognized him except my son."

The Reguleses recall that several performers, including Lee Greenwood and B.J. Thomas, remembered them later on. Most of the entertainers, they say, were easy to work with.

"The Pointer Sisters were great. They wanted Pat to go on tour with them!" Kathy remembered.

With the help of Joyce Martin, a booking agent, the committee had good choices for its entertainment.

Phyllis Hendrix, a past president of the festival and the sponsorship coordinator, recalled several years when entertainers brought huge crowds.

In 1988, right as her fame was peaking, Gloria Estefan played the Marion Popcorn Festival.

"When you stood on the stage and looked out, it was nothing but people," Hendrix said. "It was amazing. They couldn't even drive up Church Street [in downtown Marion] and make that turn because the people were just jammed in there. When we booked her, she still hadn't hit."

Regules said booking Estefan was his "crowning achievement" as president. He recalls having to borrow a stage set and lighting equipment from someone in Detroit to fit the specifications of Estefan's new show, as she had changed it between the time the festival booked her and the time she was there to play.

REO Speedwagon was another huge hit, with the crowd stretching as far as the eye could see.

Hendrix said The Pointer Sisters, who played in 1984, also came in under the radar—the festival committee booked them before they got famous, but they were a huge hit by the time September 1984 rolled around.

"It's amazing backstage the difference in the entertainers; 85 to 90 percent of them are wonderful to work with," she said.

Behind the Scenes

Pat Regules is still a mainstay behind the stage at the festival. And there is a lot to do for the entertainers beyond stage setup and teardown. The performers need food, they need hotel rooms and some of them request special snacks and drinks.

"It gets grueling," he said. "It's not an easy job."

For his wife, the festival is a week when she doesn't see him much.

"He would leave Tuesday morning, and I wouldn't see him again until Saturday night," Kathy added. "Or Sunday morning, by the time he got home. I mean, I'd see him at the festival, but…"

Immediately after the last show on Saturday, Pat is ready with his crew of helpers to get that stage torn down. He said one of the first things the festival founders decided on was to make sure the roads were cleaned up by Sunday morning.

Another main part of the entertainment portion of the festival is funding. For a while, Regules said, the Kroger Corporation was a major sponsor and brought in tens of thousands of dollars to put on shows. These days, with less funding coming in, the festival relies on several outside events to bring in more cash. Though entertainers and the cost of hosting them gets more expensive every year, the committees still manage to pull together and get known acts from across the country.

Something for Everyone

Mike Nicolosi remembers a certain entertainment format for the first few years.

"Thursday night's entertainment would be more oriented toward seniors. We would have accordion players, we'd have something on at the smaller beer gardens, we'd have something on the main stage and then on down at the Palace [Theater] so we could kind of capture the seniors and bring them in.

"Friday early on was—it started out as country, and Saturday was pop. Because of scheduling and so forth, that's changed around."

He said the festival has been fortunate to have groups that "had high energy levels."

Local bands also perform at the festival along with national acts. *Marion Popcorn Festival.*

The festival has hosted artists for all generations and all music tastes. *Marion Popcorn Festival.*

Crowds like this one from 1995 often fill the streets around the stage. *Wyandot Popcorn Museum.*

Two members of Pleasant High School's Spartans in Motion enjoy snow cones at the festival. *Marion Popcorn Festival.*

In recent years, the committee has followed a certain format: a tribute band and/or local name, a pop/rock group and a country group.

Karen Herr has served as the festival's publicity chair for more than twenty years and says the variety of entertainment is impressive.

"When you look at the size of Marion and you look at that list of entertainers and what they've been able to accomplish with no repeat entertainment for thirty-four years, [it] is absolutely awesome," she said.

Herr said the festival committee will continue to keep a diverse group of entertainers on stage, even as prices continue to rise for big-ticket performers. She said she enjoys the tribute bands because many of them aren't used to playing for such a big crowd—they bring an exciting energy to Marion.

The Showcase Stage features local entertainers all weekend—bands, cheerleaders, dancers, choirs, et cetera, all in attendance to entertain Marion crowds. This, of course, draws friends and family to see the show.

"We wanted to spread the capability of the festival to provide something for all ages," Regules said.

Chapter 6

PARADES AND PAGEANTS

Since the first festival, the popcorn pageants have expanded to include everyone from toddlers to married women. The Poppin' Pooch Pageant was even established to showcase the cutest dog in the county.

Other pageants (Little Wee Pop, Wee Pop, Teen Pop, Teeny Pop, Miss Popcorn, Ms. Popcorn) offer an opportunity for young women to vie for a crown—and the young women in Miss and Ms. Popcorn even have scholarship opportunities and chances to compete in other pageants if they win. And as a boost to attendance, friends and family members will come to watch the girls and young women compete for the crown.

The first Popcorn Queen still lives and works in Marion and has seen the growth of the festival and the pageant she took part in thirty-four years ago.

Armed with agricultural knowledge and a love for Marion, Lynn Zucker (maiden name Loudenslager) took home the first Popcorn Queen crown.

At the time, the festival had only the Miss Popcorn contest and a Teeny Pop contest. The pageants were a last-minute decision on the board's part.

"I heard about it on the radio," said Zucker, recalling that she wore a red sundress to the competition.

There were about twenty or thirty other girls in the competition, and they all had an interview session in the basement of what is now 5/3 Bank in Marion, near Marion Technical College. For Zucker, whose family still owns a farm, this was an opportunity to promote her hometown.

And since her mom worked in the employment office, she knew firsthand how downtrodden some people were because of local businesses going out of town.

A dog in an Ohio State University uniform participates in the Poppin' Pooch Pageant. *Marion Popcorn Festival.*

Popcorn royalty hanging out in 2000. *Wyandot Popcorn Museum.*

Mr. and Miss Wee Pop 2011 walk onto the stage. *Marion Popcorn Festival.*

"We had 150 years, almost, of glory years, so to speak," she said. "Really, in the late '70s, things got really rough and really bad, and it did in a lot of places."

She had never been a pageant girl, but she was determined to show the judges her passion for Marion and for farming.

"I thought, 'Oh, we're going to be promoting the popcorn industry here in Marion and the agricultural aspect of it and then the processing that we had," she said. "I had been the Marion County Beef Queen [at the county fair], so I was always very much a promoter of the agricultural industry."

Though her family didn't grow popcorn, they did grow feed corn—and Zucker was prepared to answer any corn questions she could. She said she remembers telling the judges about the moisture in popcorn kernels and how the kernels pop. As an agriculture major at Ohio State University, farming was something she was used to talking about. She was crowned queen at the Marion County Courthouse, about a week before the first festival.

These days, some of the winners get pretty nice prizes. Zucker's prize? A T-shirt and ten free car washes.

"I made sure to go out the next year and get prize packs," she said.

Big winnings or no, Zucker said she enjoyed herself.

"For me, it was just a blast to get to be part of something that was the first thing," she said. "To know that it was the first one and not know if it was going to go on. But of course, at that time, I always thought it was."

That first year, no one knew what to expect of the festival as a whole, let alone what to expect from its first queen. But Zucker said she was bound and determined to welcome people to Marion.

"I basically tried to meet all of the vendors and welcome them…I believe that they had a craft show and an art show the first year, so I tried to meet and greet the people," she said.

A highlight for her was getting to meet—and even sing for—The Lettermen. There wasn't a talent portion of the pageant that first year, but she says Mike Nicolosi told the band that their Popcorn Queen was a darn good singer.

"I sang the first thing that came to my mind, which, believe it or not, was 'Rocky Top,'" she said.

Zucker is now the executive director of Habitat for Humanity of Marion County, and she said she credits her festival experiences for helping her make connections in the community.

"I really look at it as a watershed moment in my life, a lot of it because of the contacts that I made and the folks that I got to know," she said. "Really, as I've gone through, there's so many folks that I got to know that have had an influence on job opportunities and that kind of thing."

Popcorn Festival royalty take a break at the 2007 festival. *Marion Popcorn Festival.*

Zucker said she has been volunteering off and on with the festival, judging a few pageants since she became queen and being designated "Queen Mother." At important anniversaries, the festival board asks her to come back and help celebrate. And at the first Ms. Popcorn pageant in 2009, Zucker took home another crown.

"My kids always tell me there should be a 'Granny Pop,'" she laughed.

Down the Road

Of course, as the first queen (or first Miss Marion Popcorn), Zucker was in the inaugural Popcorn Festival parade. She recalls riding in a renovated Duesenberg that first year, but she has been in several parades since then—as a member of her church, as a member of the Ridgedale Future Farmers of America and as a returning Miss (and Ms.) Marion Popcorn.

"It's all been fun," she said, adding that the parade is her favorite part of the year's festivities.

The annual ride through Marion is one of the festival's most well-attended events, and people stake out their spots early for parade seating. Lawn chairs crop up along the sidewalks on Monday or Tuesday.

Kids hang out the window to say hello during a Popcorn Festival parade. *Marion Popcorn Festival.*

People line up their chairs to watch the Popcorn Festival Parade early on in the week, but these people have made it to Thursday night. *Marion Popcorn Festival.*

"There's something kind of electric about the parade for me," Zucker said. "There's just kind of a feel in the air."

And since 1981, she said, she has been to every festival and almost every parade.

Over the years, the parade has had some very noteworthy grand marshals and marchers, including "Jungle" Jack Hanna of the Columbus Zoo, the Ohio State University mascot, local television personalities, politicians and more. And with a different theme every year, each float has the

Brutus Buckeye, the Ohio State University mascot, dances in the Marion Popcorn Festival parade. *Marion Popcorn Festival.*

ConAgra Snack Foods celebrates a tiki-themed parade. *Marion Popcorn Festival.*

These people are celebrating twenty years of "Poppin' Good Times" in 2000. *Wyandot Popcorn Museum.*

opportunity to be creative—whether the theme is "Storybook Land," "The Popcorn Olympics," "Operation Popcorn" or one of the many other themes that have surfaced throughout the years.

Zucker said one of her favorite parts about the festival, and especially the parade, is that familiar faces are everywhere.

"If you're in the parade, you see folks you know. If you're not in the parade, you're standing there watching, and you see folks you know," she said. "Either way, it's fun."

Delaney Drew, a 2008 Marion Harding High School graduate, said the parade has always been her favorite thing about the festival.

"When I was in elementary up through about middle school, my parents would get my brother and I up early before school to go set out our chairs on Center Street to save our spots to watch the parade that evening," she remembered. "It was a family tradition to watch the parade together with our dogs, then head down to the festival for dinner. We would stand along Center Street and shout out to the people we knew."

And they weren't just watching; they were trying to decide who had the best presentation.

"We'd critique the floats. It was like my family were *American Idol* judges or something…voting on whose float was the most creative and which participants weren't enthusiastic enough."

Chapter 7

SOMETHING TO BE PROUD OF

A Point of Pride

Many of the festival's faithful visitors and volunteers have a special perspective on the festival: they have lived in the city or county their entire lives.

For Lynn Zucker, who said she used to read county history books as a young girl, there is a lot to celebrate in her hometown. The Popcorn Festival is one of many.

"I love it, I really love it when our hometown folks are getting out there and being vendors, whether it's a school booster club or whether it's a local restaurant," she said. "It gives people a chance to have a taste of Marion and be a part of that.

"I love this town. There are so many positive things."

Pat Regules, a lifelong Marion County resident, echoed these statements when he said that Marion residents have more to celebrate than a once-a-year festival.

"Basically, we wanted to do something for Marion, to bring up the prominence of Marion and what we have to offer here," he said. "The fact that President Harding was born here, his house is still here and a lot of things you don't really realize we still have here."

Younger Marionites also see a local impact from the festival. Marion native Hank Owings, who graduated from Marion Harding High School in 2010, said he has fond memories of the Popcorn Festival as a young boy.

A view from above the festival. *Marion Popcorn Festival.*

A crowd of people eat and mingle at the 1995 Marion Popcorn Festival. *Wyandot Popcorn Museum.*

"15 Years of Poppin' Fun" float at the 1995 festival. *Wyandot Popcorn Museum.*

"I went like every year with my mom or friends," he said. "It was like the essential thing to do in the fall."

As an adult, he said he sees the festival's benefits to his hometown.

"I think it's a pretty good thing for Marion, along with the [Marion County] fair and the Festival on the Green," he said. "Public events like that are what not only get the community together but also make the factory-farming town a lot more 'alive.'"

Owings is moving to Chicago this fall to pursue his master's degree and an eventual doctorate, so he may not be at festivals in the near future. But some people he meets in graduate school, especially if they are from Ohio, might know about where he's from. Owings said many people from out of town know Marion for the festival and its farming history, as well as the county's connection to Warren G. Harding.

Delaney Drew also said she has grown to appreciate the festival as she's gotten older and had the opportunity to hang out with her friends on the midway.

"I also remember the first time my parents let me go to the festival on my own with my friends," she said. "That was a big deal. Then, when I moved to college, I brought a bunch of my friends down for the festival weekend. That was cool too. It's a great way to showcase Marion and its sense of community and to get everyone downtown."

Economic Impact

Since there is no entrance gate, there is no real way to tell how many people are at the festival in any given year. In the past, the board has tried to calculate based on the number of visitors per square foot. But even if there are only a few thousand people from out of town, that means a few thousand people need hotel rooms and gas and that they might be looking for something else to do while they're in Marion.

Diane Watson, executive director at the Marion County Convention and Visitors Bureau, said the festival is definitely a boon for the local economy.

"The hotels may not fill up completely, but we do get pretty full based on the entertainer," she said. "There are a lot of people who come to town and spend money with the vendors downtown. And the vendors spend their money at local retailers."

She said that the Wyandot Popcorn Museum is very popular during the festival and praised George Brown for his work putting it together.

"It's quite a drawing point for the community," she said.

Watson said the festival attendance fluctuates based on the main stage entertainment, but the fact that it's free really draws people in.

And besides the festival and the museum, there are plenty of other attractions in Marion: the Warren G. Harding Memorial and Harding Home,

A customer at one of many food vendors. *Marion Popcorn Festival.*

the Huber Machinery Museum, the Marion Union Station Museum, the Buckeye Telephone Museum and several other local attractions. Throughout the year, the Convention and Visitors Bureau sees a number of tour groups come in to spend a day in the county.

Karen Herr manages Downtown Marion, Incorporated. In this capacity and with her work as Popcorn Festival publicity chair, she has quite a bit of knowledge about how the festival impacts the downtown area.

Business for downtown shops is different during festival days, she says.

"It's almost all local people Thursday and Friday during the day," Herr said. "The out-of-town people come in Saturday and Sunday."

People who normally eat and drink downtown will be spending their dollars with food vendors. But, Herr said, the vendors themselves enjoy eating locally while they're in town. There are a good handful of restaurants within walking distance of the festival's epicenter.

"They eat fair food all the time," Herr said, adding that Marion's Candy Shack and Café even offers to deliver meals to the vendors.

Herr said it's hard to track the impact that vendors and visitors have in town—people who fill up at local gas stations, vendors who get produce at the supermarket and anyone who might need to swing by the drugstore to buy aspirin are all giving money back to Marion.

Also, though out-of-town visitors may get their fill of food at the festival, they also stop by the locally owned shops while they're in Marion. Some stores downtown will stay open late, and Herr said the visitors often head to these businesses while they wait for their favorite artists to play on the main stage.

She said it's important for people in Marion to take pride in their city.

Watson said there is a lot of local pride in the festival and that people who live in the county look forward to it every year.

"We own it," she said. "It's definitely a part of Marion. We've championed popcorn. It's an industry that's done very well here."

Herr said the festival gives Marion residents a positive thing to be proud of, as it has done since the 1980s, when it started.

Marion mayor Scott Schertzer was a teenager when the Popcorn Festival began and now sees it through the eyes of a city leader and a dad to two young girls. He has been in city government for fifteen years, serving as a city councilman before taking the mayor's seat in 2008.

He said there is something for "every age group and every generation" at the festival. As a young man, Schertzer worked in the political sector in Columbus. He said people would always know about the Popcorn Festival.

Pop P. Corn gets ready to kick off a run at the 2007 festival. *Marion Popcorn Festival.*

"They knew about the festival and the quality entertainment," he said. "They knew it was free. It's a source of pride."

Schertzer said he remembers fondly when the woman who is now his wife was the Popcorn Festival Queen in 1996.

"I remember how I thought she was beautiful," he said. "I didn't know her then. I didn't meet her until a few years later."

Now, he and his wife, Ann, are seeing their daughters Sydney and Olivia enjoy the festival, and their favorite activities have changed as they have grown up.

"When my girls were smaller, they wanted to go ride the rides," he said. "As they are getting into middle school, they're meeting their friends, they're walking around and hanging out. That's how I remember it. It was a good event to go to with your friends. As they mature, they'll get more into the entertainment."

Of course, his daughters get a little closer to the entertainers since they come to the festival with the mayor of Marion.

"My girls have an advantage that their dad is the mayor. They get to meet the entertainment in person," he said. "They think that's pretty cool. They were familiar with Grace Potter when she came."

The Marion Harding High School cheerleaders and their mascot march in the parade. *Marion Popcorn Festival.*

Being mayor, Schertzer looks at things differently than an average citizen might. He said he is always concerned about how to manage the taxpayer expense to the festival; the city provides extra police, fire and EMS service during the three days of the festival.

"Of course, I have to look at a mayor's perspective, as taxpayers scrutinize how governments and people spend dollars," he said. "The local government has the responsibility to participate but also manage the taxpayers' expense.

"The current board works with us to reduce the cost of the festival and provide a real quality festival here in downtown Marion," he continued. "We're doing things much smarter than we used to."

He said he will continue to make sure the festival is a good experience for citizens and out-of-towners.

"I will look back fondly on the Popcorn Festivals when I was mayor," he said.

A Downtown Fixture

As the festival started, Marion was in a bit of an economic downturn. And in the past few years, the city has been hit by the 2008 recession and some cuts to local government funding. Nicolosi said the festival soldiers on year after year and gives Marion something to look forward to.

"Marion struggled [when the festival started]. It's still a great community; it's got a great workforce, it's a wonderful work ethic. We've got some major employers, not like we used to."

Local business owners and people like Karen Herr work to keep money and jobs in the downtown area, he said.

"There's been a big, in the last fifteen to twenty years, a concentrated effort to bring downtown Marion…not back to life, but *to* life. People are keeping the hope alive that Marion will come back, that downtown Marion will come back to a certain level."

Regules said the money coming in is important for downtown.

"Any major event brings in money related to people spending it for different things," he said. "It exposes some of the businesses downtown."

In the past, there have been people who asked to move the Popcorn Festival out of downtown. The Marion County Fairgrounds are just a few blocks away, as is Veterans Memorial Coliseum. But that, Nicolosi and Herr said, would change the entire aesthetic.

The "Wyandot Tiki Bar" rolls through town during the parade in 2007. *Marion Popcorn Festival.*

An overhead view of the Marion Popcorn Festival as people decide what to eat. *Marion Popcorn Festival.*

Popcorn royalty get ready to kick off a run at the 2010 Marion Popcorn Festival. *Marion Popcorn Festival.*

"It's to showcase Marion, showcase our downtown," Nicolosi said. "It would no longer be a street festival [if we moved it]."

Current president Karen Shaffer echoed this statement.

"It would die outside of the downtown," she said. "It's not a fair…it's a street festival."

Chapter 8

LOOKING BACK, LOOKING FORWARD

Keeping Interest High

Karen Shaffer, who will finish her term as festival president in 2014, said the festival has been well attended since its inception—but recent years haven't brought crowds like in years past.

"You could barely walk through it some nights," she said, recalling how packed the streets were in the 1990s. "We have had those nights [lately], but not like every night."

She said there was an attendance drop-off when the recession hit around 2007 or 2008. But part of the reason might also be that today's teenagers have so many extracurriculars going on—Friday nights at the festival may have lower attendance, for example, because people are out at high school football games.

"What we're seeing now is people making choices as to whether the kids ride rides all day long or they eat. I mean, they're using money frugally…don't think that any festival you go to anymore, the crowds are like what they used to be. And I attribute that to the fact that teenagers these days are so busy."

And in a few years, the teenagers in school plays and on the football field will be the ones the festival committee is counting on to take over.

"We're getting a few [younger people]," Shaffer said. "We are trying to bring our part of the festival into the century of social media."

Shaffer said the festival is making other strides, such as being able to accept credit card payments for some vendors. And with a new website

Crowds gather on the street at the 1995 festival. *Marion Popcorn Festival.*

A group of local veterans waves from a parade float. *Marion Popcorn Festival.*

upgrade and a social media presence, as well as a continued lineup of name entertainment, the crowds will probably just keep coming.

"The parade is still well attended, it's just that the '90s compared to now is a big difference," Shaffer said. "But I think that can be said about many things."

People like Hank Owings are the ones getting involved with the festival now—men and women in their twenties. He said he knows people in the community who will be willing to take up the mantle as the original festival crowd gets older.

"I know a handful of churches in Marion that are deeply invested in the community, and I could see a few people of various ages associated with those communities having a hand in continuing it—if they chose to," he said. "And there are people at OSUM [Ohio State University–Marion] and MTC [Marion Technical College] who will be in Marion for quite a while who probably would also be interested."

Maintaining the Theme

Something the festival board and past leaders hear often is this question: "Where's the popcorn?" The salty snack isn't on every corner, as some visitors might expect.

"The theme has been hard to maintain," Nicolosi said.

Buckets of popcorn at the 2005 Marion Popcorn Festival. *Marion Popcorn Festival.*

Festival-goers enjoy a picnic. *Marion Popcorn Festival.*

At an apple festival, you can sample apple pie, apple butter, apple cider, apple-glazed meats and more. Same with a pumpkin festival—pumpkin pie, pumpkin bread, pumpkin spice coffee, pumpkin soup. At a bratwurst festival, you can get a bratwurst or at least a sausage sandwich at almost every concession stand.

Cyclists make their way through Marion for the 2009 Popcorn 100.
Marion Popcorn Festival.

But at the Popcorn Festival, it is a little harder to maintain the theme within the concessions. Popcorn bread or a popcorn coffee probably wouldn't be appealing to everyone, so there aren't popcorn vendors as far as the eye can see at the Marion Popcorn Festival.

Nicolosi said the festival has tried to incorporate the food in many different ways over the last thirty-four years, but at the end of the day, if you're walking

People line up for mini doughnuts at the 2010 festival. *Marion Popcorn Festival.*

around in the hot sun for several hours, you'll probably get more mileage out of a steak sandwich than you will out of a shovelful of popcorn.

That doesn't mean there aren't popcorn vendors; they are definitely on the streets along with the other concessionaires. And almost everything else, from the pageants to the sporting events, has a popcorn name or theme.

The winner of each pageant, from Wee Pop to Ms. Popcorn, holds a popcorn-themed royal title. The Popcorn 100 bike ride, Poppin' Pins Bowling Tournament, Popcorn Bowl Football Tournament and more provide entertainment and competition opportunities for the festival crowds.

So, Nicolosi said, future Popcorn Festival leaders will have to make sure the theme carries on.

Future Goals

Castanien said that in the beginning, the festival founders "couldn't imagine" their brainchild still being a thriving event almost thirty-five years later.

Looking forward, she said, her goals are pretty clear.

A woman waves from the HER Realty float. *Wyandot Popcorn Museum.*

Ronald McDonald and Pop P. Corn make a presentation. *Marion Popcorn Festival.*

"We just want to have a good festival every year," she said, adding that she hopes more volunteers will join the festival family.

Herr said she wants to make sure the festival continues to be enjoyable for everyone in Marion.

"We want to continue to provide people a place that they can have fun and forget," she said, adding that local people love coming to the festival to see old friends. "We want to continue to make an impact on Marion in a positive way."

Herr also said she wants to make sure the festival continues to have money to bring good entertainers into town.

Nicolosi echoed Herr's statements about the festival being a time when people can be carefree and enjoy themselves.

"We always try to keep the main focus on bringing something to the community," he said. "Even when times are bad, this is three days they can kind of forget, relax, come down and have a good time."

Of course, it's not just Marionites who show up on the weekend after Labor Day.

"People look forward to it. When they know the Popcorn Festival is coming up, they come from all over. The fact that they get to see people they haven't seen for years, it's like a big reunion!"

Popcorn 100 participants work their way through their bike course. *Marion Popcorn Festival.*

And in his eyes, it's something that is going to keep going for many years to come.

"It has taken on a life of its own," he said. "I don't see it going away anytime in the near future."

More Information

Marion Public Library
445 East Church Street
Marion, Ohio 43302
(740) 387-0992
http://www.marion.lib.oh.us

Wyandot Popcorn Museum
169 East Church Street
Marion, Ohio 43302
(740) 387-4255
http://www.wyandotpopcornmus.com

Marion Popcorn Festival
PO Box 1101
Marion, Ohio 43301-1101
(740) 387-FEST or (740) 387-3378
E-mail: marionpopcornfestival@gmail.com
www.popcornfestival.com

Marion History Museum
169 East Church Street
Marion, Ohio 43302
(740) 387-4255
Fax: (740) 387-0117
E-mail: mchs@marionhistory.com
http://www.marionhistory.com

Chapter 9

CREATIVE SNACKERS AND POPCORN'S FUTURE

Popcorn in America

Corn was first domesticated in the Americas in Mexico about 9,000 years ago. A recent archaeological find points to evidence that people in ancient Peru ate popcorn more than 6,500 years ago—of course, with no microwaves, they possibly just held the corn over an open flame and waited for the kernels to pop. The world's oldest popcorn popper dates to about 300 BC.[20]

Spanish explorers and missionaries wrote about popcorn's importance to native Latin American tribes, including its place in early ceremonies. Writing of Peruvian Indians in 1650, missionary Bernabé Cobo says, "They toast a certain kind of corn until it bursts. They call it *pisancalla*, and they use it as a confection." Indigenous people in Peru ate popcorn or used ground maize for flour. It is likely that people in other regions of the Americas enjoyed the food, too.[21]

Many stories about the Aztecs using popcorn revolve around religion and rituals. Franciscan missionary Bernardino de Sahagún wrote about such a ceremony: "And also a number of young women danced, having so vowed, a popcorn dance. As thick as tassels of maize were their popcorn garlands. And these they placed upon [the girls'] heads."

In 1519, conquistador Hernán Cortés got his first sight of popcorn when he invaded Mexico and came into contact with the Aztecs, as Sahagún had. The Aztecs used popcorn as decoration for ceremonial headdresses, necklaces and ornaments on statues of their gods, including Tlaloc, the god of rain and fertility. An early Spanish account of a ceremony honoring the Aztec gods who watched over fishermen reads: "They scattered before him parched corn, called *momochitl*, a kind of corn which bursts when parched and discloses its contents and makes itself look like a very white flower; they said these were hailstones given to the god of water."[22]

Corn made its way up to the United States and was a widely planted crop in the 1800s.

Creative Recipes

Before movie theatres and carnivals made popcorn a household snack, the food had a place in nineteenth- and twentieth-century cookbooks as an additive to just about anything. Sam Nelson Jr.'s popcorn company in Grinnell, Iowa, printed a pamphlet in 1916 and suggested putting popped corn in omelets, hash, custard, macaroons and pie and serving it with roasts, cutlets, parsnips, turnips, carrots, macaroni, potatoes and prunes. The company also recommended it for use in soups, salads and confections.[23]

Native Americans and European colonists ate ground corn mush with breakfast, but popped corn was also made into popcorn pudding, whether whole or ground up. An 1858 recipe included three pints of milk, two eggs, three pints of popcorn and some salt, mixed together and baked for half an hour before being served with a thick cream. Raw and popped corn pudding faded after World War I, but ground popcorn flour resurfaced after the end of World War II, when America sent other grains to Europe. A bad freeze in 1947 destroyed much of the popcorn crop, halting the sales of popcorn bread and popcorn muffins out of Chicago.[24]

Prior to World War I, popcorn was also a breakfast treat, served as a hot or cold cereal with cream and sugar and perhaps a little fruit or just submerged in milk. Again, the fad petered out before the Second World War and saw a small resurgence when other grains were sent overseas.[25]

Popcorn balls, which are still a treat today, were introduced in the mid- to late 1800s. They were difficult to make at home, which possibly led to a decrease in popularity, but people could find them at amusement parks and fairs, including Coney Island. Some people would add chocolate, vanilla, peppermint or honey to the popcorn balls for some excitement.[26]

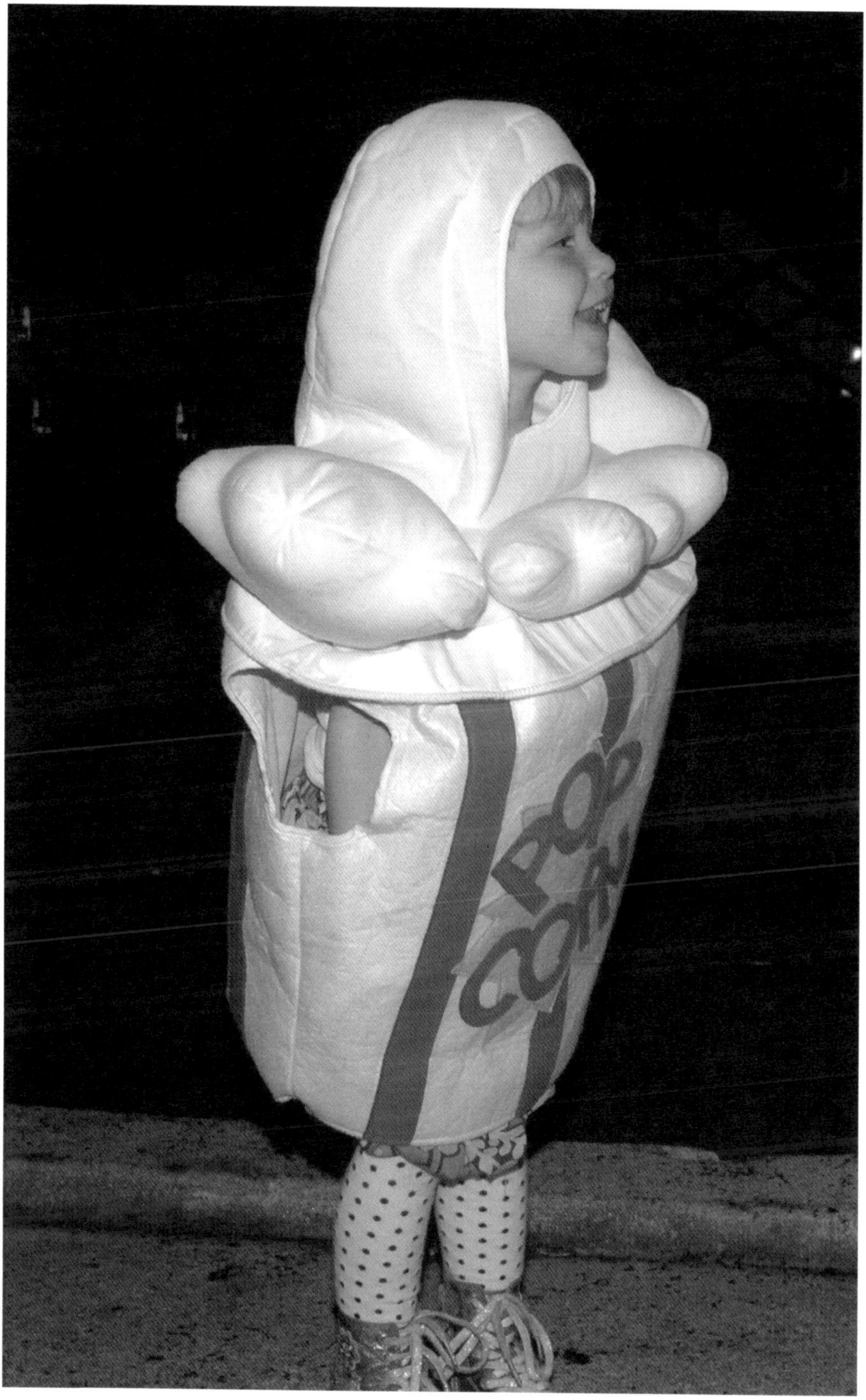

A little bucket of corn enjoys the festival. *Marion Popcorn Festival.*

Other popped recipes included popcorn cakes, flattened corn crisps and crispettes and popcorn candy. Some inventive cooks even recommended using popcorn as a garnish on soups or salads.[27]

As companies like Wyandot, Incorporated, and Cracker Jack can attest, flavored popcorn is one novelty that doesn't seem to be going away anytime soon. Although popcorn recipes died out around the early 1900s, popcorn by itself saw a huge spike in popularity during the time of the Great Depression. It was one of the few things that many could afford during the Depression; it cost only about five or ten cents a bag. While other businesses failed, the popcorn business saw growth—as W. Hoover Brown and Ava Brown learned.

During World War II, sugar was sent overseas for U.S. troops, which meant there wasn't much sugar left in the States to make candy. Americans ate triple the amount of popcorn during the war years.

Popcorn sales in the theater went into a slump during the early 1950s, when television became popular. When people began eating popcorn at home, the new relationship between television and popcorn led to an uptick in popularity.[28]

See popcorn recipes in Appendix B.

Popcorn Poppers

Charles Cretors is credited for starting the popper industry, but many companies behind him adapted and changed his "recipe."

Fred (best known as Jake) Hoke and James Holcomb started the Holcomb & Hoke Manufacturing Company in 1914 and made machines until 1934, when the Great Depression really took hold. They sold machines called BUTTER-KIST, mostly to drugstores, five-and-dime stores, candy stores, theaters, department stores and bars.

The process included dumping a set amount of kernels into the popper, agitating it, popping it, removing unpopped kernels, buttering it and dumping it out after it was done popping. The smaller counter models were also fully automatic except for adding the oil. Neither model salted the corn.

All BUTTER-KIST popcorn machines were highly polished sparkling nickel plate (later models) or German silver (earlier models), according to the Wyandot Popcorn Museum. The cabinets were wooden, finished in either rich mahogany, natural oak color or a darker color.[29]

The Burch and Manley Company came along in the 1920s, though founders J.R. Burch and Charles T. Manley eventually split off and made separate companies. The Wyandot Popcorn Museum has a 1932 Burch World's Fair model; a popper from Manley, Inc.; and a popper from the Star Manufacturing Company, which Burch founded after he split with Manley.[30]

As Paul Newman made a foray into popcorn in 1982, he chose Wyandot as the distributor of his jar-packed Newman's Own Popcorn. Newman wanted a historic wagon to promote the popcorn at a media event in New York, and the folks at Wyandot knew just the one. The Dunbar wagon they had in mind was the work of inventor Charles Dunbar, who worked with Charles Cretors but had a different view for his machines:

> *Paul called Wyandot and wanted to acquire an Antique Wagon to promote his popcorn at the media event and later at supermarkets and in Central Park in NYC. We knew Dennis Koepsell owned the best preserved Dunbar Antique Wagon in Milwaukee, Wisc. Paul arranged to rent the wagon for the media event, and then later bought the wagon from Dennis. Getting it in Central Park was quite another thing. He used all his prestige and influence and finally succeeded by donating all the profit to the disadvantaged children of the inner city…*
>
> *A horse trailer was built especially for the antique to keep it safe from vandals when not in use. Paul paid Mr. Koepsell over $20,000 plus the cost of the trailer. Despite this precaution, major vandalism occurred, and a local firm was hired to repair the damage. They really were not qualified, and the results ruined the appearance and cost much extra to restore later on by Wyandot Popcorn Museum.*
>
> *In 1987, Paul contacted Wyandot with a desire to sell the antique. It was bought by George Brown, and then two years later donated to the Museum. At that time the Museum was located in the Perry Bed & Breakfast on S. State Street, and the large antiques such as the Model TT Truck and the Dunbar were stored in George K. Brown's barn.*
>
> *When the Museum moved to Heritage Hall in 1989, the building was remodeled to accommodate these large vehicles with two large overhead doors, and a portable ramp.*
>
> *When Newman acquired the Dunbar antique, three large crates of original operating parts were offered in case anyone wanted to fully restore the wagon to its original condition. Wyandot suggested these parts be retained by the Popcorn Museum, so they would not be lost*

in New York City. Years later the Dunbar was gifted to the Wyandot Popcorn Museum so the crates of dry popper, boiler, butter applicator etc. were available for restoration.[31]

Of course, these machines seem antiquated next to the microwaves and large-scale movie theater poppers that people are used to today, but they were an important part of popcorn's early story and its growth.

Popcorn Today

What is the future of this beloved snack? Will it continue to be delivered in heaping helpings at movie theaters and ballgames? Or will another snack come along and push popcorn out of the running for America's fan favorite?

Recent Popcorn Trends

- Americans today consume sixteen billion quarts of popped popcorn each year. The average American eats about fifty-one quarts.[32]
- Microwave popcorn became popular in the 1980s. Today, approximately 70 percent of popcorn is eaten in the home.
- People in the United States consume the most popcorn worldwide.
- Major popcorn-producing states are Illinois, Indiana, Iowa, Kansas, Kentucky, Michigan, Missouri, Nebraska and Ohio.[33]
- At least six localities (all in the United States of America) claim to be the "Popcorn Capital of the World": Valparaiso, Indiana; Van Buren, Indiana; Marion, Ohio; Ridgway, Illinois; Schaller, Iowa; and North Loup, Nebraska. According to the USDA, most of the maize used for popcorn production is specifically planted for this purpose.[34]

Andrew F. Smith remarks on the future of popcorn in his 1999 book *Popped Culture*:

> *With popcorn sales sluggish, with health concerns challenging both microwave and theater popcorn, with dizzying corporate takeovers regularly rocking the industry, and with research declining, some observers have wondered whether or not popcorn will survive. Reports of popcorn's demise are greatly exaggerated. New technological advancements, such as the Internet, may assist popcorn in its drive for continued stardom in the snack world. Popcorn may be a mature industry in America, but it has just begun to expand abroad. The reasons for its potential success abroad are the same ones that produced popcorn's success in North America. It is easily grown, inexpensive to buy, and accessible to most people. It is readily processed and almost effortlessly prepared for consumption. It is a healthy food. As American snack foods continue their rise in popularity around the world, popcorn will follow. With the vast increase of microwave ovens in other countries, microwave popcorn will be a logical partner.*
>
> *Whatever its future abroad, popcorn remains a significant food in the United States and Canada. Perhaps popcorn as a snack food has limited growth potential for the future. Popcorn as an ingredient in cooking has just been revived and may well point in different directions for the future. Its bland taste provides a good vehicle for all types of flavors and ingredients. Its culinary versatility permits integration with almost any cuisine. Its popping still enthralls observers, young and old. Its aroma is heavenly. Popcorn is America's gift to the world, and what a wonderful, fun-filled banquet it is.*[35]

Since Smith published his book, the popcorn industry has declined a bit, but sales in pounds of unpopped popcorn still hover around one billion pounds per year as of 2012.[36]

Since 2013, the industry has seen an uptick in sales due to one thing in particular: gourmet popcorn. The $1 billion industry has changed with the introduction of new and exciting flavors: black truffle, wasabi, beer, bacon, cinnamon, Sriracha hot sauce and other flavors way beyond liquid butter and cheese dust. These gourmet bags are going for $4 or more at specialty shops.[37]

Some also herald popcorn as a health food, as it is low calorie when prepared a certain way. In March 2012, health food analyst Joe Vinson told attendees at the American Chemical Society's national meeting that popcorn hulls are good sources of fiber and polyphenols (antioxidants). In fact, he said, popcorn hulls have more of these antioxidants than many fruits and vegetables.

"Popcorn may be the perfect snack food," he said, according to *Science Daily*. "It's the only snack that is 100 percent unprocessed whole grain. All other grains are processed and diluted with other ingredients, and although cereals are called 'whole grain,' this simply means that over 51 percent of the weight of the product is whole grain. One serving of popcorn will provide more than 70 percent of the daily intake of whole grain. The average person only gets about half a serving of whole grains a day, and popcorn could fill that gap in a very pleasant way."

Vinson said that the way people prepare and serve popcorn can quickly pack on calories and fat. Cook it in a pot full of oil, slather on butter or the "liquid butter used in many movie theaters," pour on the salt or eat it as kettle corn or caramel corn with extra sugar and it can quickly weigh someone down.

"Air-popped popcorn has the lowest number of calories, of course," Vinson said. "Microwave popcorn has twice as many calories as air-popped, and if you pop your own with oil, this has twice as many calories as air-popped popcorn. About 43 percent of microwave popcorn is fat, compared to 28 percent if you pop the corn in oil yourself."[38]

With a growing emphasis on healthy eating combined with an interest in new and exciting flavors, popcorn sales could move into uncharted territory in the next several years. Of course, beloved brands like Cracker Jack and Orville Redenbacher's remain mainstays at home, at the ballpark, at the movies and at festivals and carnivals. Countless men and women have contributed to popcorn's success, including Orville Redenbacher, Charles Cretors and W. Hoover and Ava Brown. In *Popped Culture*, Smith says the story of the industry is a truly American one, defined by persistence and ingenuity:

> *I remain fascinated by popcorn myself, as fascinated as when I was a child. Popcorn's story is an exciting tale of unexpected twists and turns that are even more amusing than the frequently regurgitated popcorn myths. It is peopled with archaeologists and anthropologists, street vendors and merchants, seedsmen and farmers, processors and grocers, nutritionists and health-food nuts, scientists and salespersons, poets and songwriters, and just plain Americans. It is a story filled with hot-shot inventors, high-flying promoters, risk-taking growers, efficiency-conscious*

processors, hard-hitting advertisers, and lip-smacking consumers—all of whom have contributed to popcorn's transformation into an American icon. As important, the popcorn story is interwoven with significant events, inventions, and social movements in American history, such as the Depression and World War II; the inventions of movies, television, and the microwave; and the rise of health-food consciousness in America. It is a story worth telling.[39]

And like popcorn, the story of the Popcorn Festival is also one worth telling and worth remembering. It is a story of ingenuity, of pride, of community, of family. It is, possibly, a story as American as popcorn itself; a story of how a community picked itself up from hard times and made something great. Its longevity means that those who were kids during the first festival are now taking their own kids and grandkids downtown to see a show and ride a few rides. And the momentum doesn't seem to be stopping anytime soon—with luck and the continued work of many volunteers, people will come to the streets of Marion every September for food, music and, of course, popcorn.

Appendix A

GEORGE BROWN'S 1981 INTERVIEW WITH ORVILLE REDENBACHER

George Brown began preparing to write a history of the popcorn industry around 1980. As part of this history, he interviewed Orville Redenbacher at his home in Coronado, California, on August 3, 1981. That interview follows, and the details are factual but are extremely comprehensive in discussing Orville's breeding activities and his work with partner Charles Bowman. The interview is reprinted here courtesy of the Wyandot Popcorn Museum.

ORVILLE: From being a County Agent in Terre Haute, Indiana, I joined Princeton Farms. Basically they were interested in acquiring the rich coal deposits near Princeton, Indiana. At that time they were the largest farm industry in Indiana. It proved easier to buy the farm to get the mineral rights than to buy the coal rights alone. With the other farmers in the area you had to get them to sell their mineral rights and many did not want to bother to do that. So, rather than waste your efforts on only buying the mineral rights, most of the time you could buy the land and rights for various amounts.
GEORGE: So that was how the Princeton Operation started down there?
ORVILLE: Yeah, well in the Depression we had to divert corn acreage. In my first year in 1940, the first thing I did was to build a Hybrid Seed Corn Plant. In 1941 I started with Hybrid Popcorn Seed at Princeton Farms.
GEORGE: Can I have a copy of this story?
ORVILLE: I kept it out for you. This has been printed since more details of it are in The People. *I'll get the reprints.*

GEORGE: You gave me a copy of this earlier. I have one [tan booklet].

ORVILLE: Take an extra if you want.

GEORGE: Since we are setting up the museum, I will take it for the character pictures.

ORVILLE: Yes.

GEORGE: Nice, who did that?

ORVILLE: Oh, that was when I was up in Toronto. They used it in the Sun Magazine *Sunday Supplement when they interviewed me for a story, and I did not even know he was doing that. They ran that in the story. I can give you a photocopy of this sketch. Hunt Wesson used the sketch to produce note paper for notes and letters that were written from time to time.*

GEORGE: Fantastic idea! You had sent me a note on that pad style a while back. It's a neat idea. Let's get back talking more about Charlie Bowman and your early popcorn history. The material that we got in recent years from Paul Cardinal, Princeton's current General Manager and his predecessor, H.B. Fulford, is too recent to have helped in telling your story at Princeton Farms. Why don't we go back to when you were a County Agent, and also get more of your educational background.

ORVILLE: Yes, after I graduated from Purdue, I taught Agriculture for one year. I then moved to Terre Haute to become an Assistant County Agent. I opened an office in Terre Haute, established eight of them, and became one of the eight.

GEORGE: That was at Terre Haute before you worked at Princeton Farms?

ORVILLE: At a little town Northeast of Terre Haute in the same County. I became a Vocational Agricultural Teacher there from July 28, 1928 to May 31, 1929. I then went into the County Agent Office as Assistant County Agent for a year and nine months. The County Agent was moved to Indianapolis so I took over as County Agent and stayed on until December 31, 1939. Since both Tony Hulman and the Smiths lived in Terre Haute, I knew and worked with them. They also owned The Indianapolis Speedway. They talked me into quitting the County Agent work and going to work with them at a pretty good increase in salary. I moved to Princeton, Indiana and became a professional Farm Manager for that operation.

GEORGE: Was it called Princeton Farms at that time?

ORVILLE: Oh, no. The original name was McDonner. Nothing there, just a crust of land. Some was owned by the Deep Vein Mine Company, some owned by Princeton Manufacturing Company, and some owned by the Smiths. All was just co-mingled.

GEORGE: What was the full name of the Smith family? I knew the Hulmans, but I am not familiar with the Smiths.

ORVILLE: Well, down there as far as they were concerned, their two big projects were the Princeton Mining Company, the biggest one. They also had Deep Vein Coal Company. The Princeton Mining Company was the one that really owned the deep shaft mine and they owned a lot more coal besides that under their 12,000 acres. They could not get the rights to this coal without buying the 12,000 acres. No, they did buy 2 or 3 small tracts to finish out certain areas. When we got to farming it became illogical to have farms here and a few acres owned by others, so some buying cleaned up this problem. We started to farm all that land with hired labor. We had at the start of World War II, 38 boys drafted off our farms before they began to exempt agricultural workers. We finally got ourselves in a bind and had to do some 50-50 tenant leases. Like I said, we in my first year there developed a hybrid seed corn plant.

GEORGE: That was your first year as the Farm Professional Manager?

ORVILLE: That was January 1, 1940, when I arrived. We grew our first Hybrid Dent Corn in 1940 and our first Hybrid Popcorn in 1941.

GEORGE: Well then the Hybrids you produced were Purdue Hybrids?

ORVILLE: Yeah, they were all Purdue Hybrids. I did not have time to produce my own. I was at Princeton 12 years until December 31, 1951.

GEORGE: Your starting in your own seed business was not a long time from when I graduated from Purdue in February 1950.

ORVILLE: You have to keep in mind that I started my first crop of Hybrid Popcorn seed in 1941. Most of this material got to Purdue via Dr. Brunson (a popcorn breeder originally from Kansas) in 1938. Up until that time, Agriculture Alumnae had tried to reproduce what Glenn Smith and Brunson had developed for Purdue.

GEORGE: Were you able to get the inbred seed later on? As we know, Agriculture Alumnae would not release inbred or single crosses for a number of years thereby financing further research from their earlier successes. Were you able in that interim to get some seed stock or inbreeds from Brunson to initiate your own research?

ORVILLE: Keep in mind that P-38, Purdue 31, and Purdue 32 were all single cross females with an inbred male. For example, on P-32, the female is Purdue 20, and on Purdue 31, the female was Purdue 22. Well, at first I couldn't get the inbreeds for Purdue, 20 or 22, but I could buy the Single Cross, and then the male inbred. So, the very first year the only Three Hybrids I could make were Purdue 31, Purdue 32, and Purdue 38.

GEORGE: They had released the inbred and the two single crosses, Purdue 20, and Purdue 22?
ORVILLE: Yes, the male inbreeds were released. So then I started going to Florida with our own nursery in the winter of 1941. We then started our own breeding but it was five or six years later that we came up with our Hybrids using materials that we could get that had potential. We then came up with Princeton Farms Hybrids in addition to producing Purdue Hybrids. Actually, we did not come up with Princeton Hybrids until 1946. Agricultural alumnae had the first Hybrids, Purdue #1 and Purdue #3. Business just flowed into them. They were the only source and they were a tax supported organization, expected to multiply the material and eventually turn it over to private firms. The Agriculture Experiment Station in Iowa at Iowa State College was doing Hybrid breeding by Dr. Eldredge. Later on his son, Crosby Eldredge, started Ames Seed Farms producing other people's hybrids and eventually via Jim Murray doing their own breeding work.
GEORGE: Packaged popcorn at that time was mostly Purdue 20?
ORVILLE: Yes, but then that soon changed. TV Time originally used Purdue 20, exclusively from Agriculture Alumnae. To save money, other cheaper to produce corns were used. Ben Banowitz, the owner, went bankrupt, to be bailed out by his brother.
GEORGE: Was it his brother?
ORVILLE: Oh, yeah, his brother was a multi-millionaire contractor. He owned many Chicago buildings and bailed him out 3 times eventually.
GEORGE: Well, I remember TV Time and the financial problems they had. I know for a time Ben Banowitz was out of the management. The CEO of TV Time, John Bishop, became President of The Popcorn Institute.
ORVILLE: That was when Ben bought that huge plant at Bremen, Indiana.
GEORGE: He used to run out of Chicago, didn't he?
ORVILLE: Yeah, he started on the 11th Floor in Chicago. We worked with him. I got acquainted with Ben when I worked at Princeton Farms and we produced all of his commercial seed. I did that in addition to the Popcorn Seed Business. When I went to Princeton, we grew all of his Purdue-20 popping corn. It was the only commercial popping corn we did.
GEORGE: Those early years when I came into the business with my Dad, TV Time was spending very heavily on TV ads in major Eastern Markets, such as New York and Philadelphia.

ORVILLE: That's one of the reasons that caused him to go broke that one time. He spent approximately $2,000.000 in advertising giving all his profits away.

GEORGE: In one year he spent over $2,000,000 on advertising?

ORVILLE: Yes.

GEORGE: I don't know about the Mary Poppins Doll Program. Why don't you tell me about that?

ORVILLE: Well, he had Mary Martin on the Peter Pan Musical, so he introduced Mary Poppins and paid a royalty to use the name. He came out with big duplicate dolls he gave to customers and famous people to promote his popcorn. He was a genius in innovative ideas, but he needed a financial manager to keep him under control. He was also a good scientist, putting together his TV Time Package with the separate pouch of Coconut Oil, since combining the two would have in a few weeks produced a soapy smell and taste. He came from the Theatre Business on the 7th Floor of South 11th Street. He had the whole enterprise up there and they developed the package just as it is today. They put corn and salt in one pouch and the oil in an adjacent pouch. Since no one else had a similar package, the equipment to manufacture it all had to be designed from scratch. He also had engineers to help him but there was no denying Ben's talent and guidance. They had used Bartlet continuous packaging for the pouches.

GEORGE: You know that Mary Poppins Box with the salt pouch at the top, built into the box. That was Ben's idea. Where did the interrelationship between H.B. Fulford and you originate? Was he with Princeton earlier in another capacity?

ORVILLE: No, Fulford was working for Igelheart, managing an elevator. I got acquainted with H.B. originally when he was a 4H Club Member, and I went down to judge the 4H animals.

GEORGE: Quoting an interview with H.B. Fulford, Redenbacher was General Manager, and H.B. came in as Asst. Mgr. and Sales Manager, aiming to expand the Hybrid Field Corn Seed Business. Fulford stayed on until he resigned to be a consultant in 1975.

ORVILLE: They called me Reddie. I mean I didn't use my first name. Most people in Terre Haute knew me as Reddie.

GEORGE: Princeton grew into the Popcorn business via the Seed route. They developed a very beautiful fiber-board can as a retail package.

ORVILLE: We started with a metal can, but due to metal shortages, changed to a paraffin coated fiber can with metal ends.

GEORGE: Okay, that's the paraffin lined that H.B. was thinking of.
ORVILLE: In 1944 and 1945 they began packing for Hulman in cans and poly bags. They sold 1, 2, and 5 lb. sizes in the poly bags. Albert Dickerson Co., started their retail packaging about the same time Princeton, Vogel, Wyandot, and Betty Zane were competing for the retail business and expanding this market. We got to know the competition very well. In the '50s popcorn made a big growth in sales from 1951 to 1960. We studied the competition carefully. Our main push was to produce the best quality and sell in quality retail outlets. Our secret was in the varieties we produced and the processing methods using ear corn drying and curing compared to the then combine harvesting by most of the others. Most of the competition was into bulk popcorn because of the major increases in the Drive-In Theatre Outlets. We chartered a plane and carefully studied all the markets we wanted to enter. This was not true of American, Betty Zane, Barteldes, TV Time Foods, to name a few exceptions. They were primarily consumer packages. The other Processors in bulk put their best quality in the bulk packs and sold inferior corn in the consumer package because many consumer buyers were only interested in a good price. The quality buyers of bulk corn booked it under contract and were very quality conscious. Princeton catered to this bulk market and had many loyal customers. The consumer package business was just getting started. In our opinion to most of the Processors, the package business was just a side issue. If they had off quality it would be channeled to the package business rather than to the bulk side of the industry. What was not good enough to sell in bulk went into the home consumption market. The quality sold in the amusement business did not measure up and that is how we [Princeton] *got into the package business with our superior product. McCarty Seed Company was one of the largest bulk operators with top integrity but not a good operator.*
ORVILLE: Fulford had been Assistant County Agent in Vincennes after graduating from Purdue. He spent many months at Igelheart.
GEORGE: And what was that type of business?
ORVILLE: They managed a string of elevators making cake flour such as Swan's Down, Fulford was manager of their receiving operation. They had 7 to 12 locations. The farmers had brought in soft wheat from Southwestern Indian and Southeastern Illinois. H.B. Fulford was managing those elevators and that is when I brought him into Princeton Farms to help out primarily with sales of Hybrid Dent Seed Corn. We grew to where we were producing nearly 600 Acres of Hybrid Dent Corn Seed yearly.

GEORGE: Were the Hybrid Dent Corn Varieties from your own breeding work?

ORVILLE: Some of the dents were from our own breeding work. We sold them under the Princeton Farms brand. We also sold some wholesale business for some of the Big Co-ops like GLS, Southern States, Central States, that were located in the East, such as New York, Pennsylvania, and the Pennsylvania Farm Bureau, and different ones like that. In 1951 and 1952 Princeton Farms produced 600 acres of Hybrid Dent Seed and about 200 acres were sold in advance.

GEORGE: About what portion was from your own production and research.

ORVILLE: We probably were producing at the end, at the time I knew, only dent seed. They didn't sell any popcorn seed in 1981 that I know of. They quit breeding Popcorn Seed after I left, and they quit producing Popcorn Seed about two years after I left. I really can't answer you too clearly. I would say that their dent seed business has tapered off. I think the big companies such as DeKalb have become too big a factor.

GEORGE: You had told me that when you went into business with Charlie Bowman that you took with you your interest in Popcorn Breeding and had gotten their Dent Corn Breeding Program off the ground. Did the dent breeding work stop after you left?

ORVILLE: No. Princeton brought in a breeder after I left there.

GEORGE: Who was the breeder? Did you know his name?

ORVILLE: They did bring in a Breeder for a while. Perhaps for two or three years. But he just did dent corn. The thing that got us into commercial popcorn at Princeton was the J.A. McCarty Seed Company who bought our seed and was one of the biggest operators in the Popcorn Industry. After we started Chester in the early '50s, J.A. McCarty bought much of his seed from Chester Hybrids. He almost went bankrupt in 1948 when high production and low prices hurt many popcorn processors. He didn't have a dryer and had a very wet season in 1974. It was very wet in southern Illinois, and Southern Indiana. I had a 28 ft. High Continuous Dryer where the shelled grain came all the way to the top and then tumbled down to the bottom, through the hot air.

GEORGE: Wouldn't you call that a batch dryer?

ORVILLE: No. It was a Continuous Dryer. I had a batch dryer also but it was for my Dent Corn. McCarty had so much wet corn that he hauled truckloads of wet corn to Valpairaso and returned to Evansville with dry popcorn. I had popcorn all over the place so I decided I might as well be in the Processing Business. One winter I dried his whole crop. We dried *continuously day and night. We had no efficient way to do it, so when we built this new popcorn plant, I went to Martin in Mansfield, Ohio, they converted their hay dryers to corn dryers, and the first steel silo they ever built was for Princeton Farms. Actually, I went back for Heavy Engineering to Purdue to help work with Martin on the strength of the duct inside. We had to change the thing at the Center. We had to make a barrier there to keep the air from by-passing. It was necessary to have an even depth of corn on the top compared to the sides, so the air would not take the easiest route and not evenly dry the stored corn. We then built a tunnel to handle the air handling and convey the corn out of the tanks as they were emptied. It was elevated by the same system used to fill the Martin Steel Ear Cribs, and then taken to the shellers and processing equipment. We designed this Princeton system with our own builders. Later on McCarty Seed Company borrowed our blueprints to build his plant at Evansville. He gave us $500 for the use of the plans. The plans were drawn up by an engineer at the Princeton Mining Company. After all, this engineer was working full time with Mrs. Hulman. He was a college graduate trained engineer.*

GEORGE: At that time McCarty had a plant in downtown Evansville, and then later he moved out into the countryside which is the place where he had the big fire.

ORVILLE: That was when he borrowed the blueprint and built a plant identical to ours but twice as big.

GEORGE: At any rate at Princeton you originally had 4 Martins and later today there are?

ORVILLE: 8 Martin ear cribs. And then they added the other Butler Bins for the shelled corn.

GEORGE: Then at McCarty Seed they put in 16 tall Martin ear popcorn Cribs?

ORVILLE: Yes.

GEORGE: Were they a double row or a single row?

ORVILLE: Single row. Princeton had the elevator on one end while McCarty had the Elevator in the center and the corn could go in both directions.

GEORGE: I saw a Bobby Ware's movie after the fire but the distortion made it hard to analyze the plant before the fire. I never saw the original plant.

ORVILLE: [Showing pictures he had with him] *That was the hybrid seed corn operation. He built that first.*

GEORGE: That burned? When did that burn?

ORVILLE: After I left Princeton. We put in a great big fan that we had taken out of the coal mine, so that we could suck air in through the exhaust via the tunnel. We used the same tunnel to carry the corn outside as you would convey coal in mining tunnels. Then the popcorn would be carried to the top of the elevator where we had mounted a sheller to shell the popcorn. The cobs were delivered to a big pile. We were one of the first to feed corn cobs to cattle. It was about the same time that Garst out of True Rapids, Iowa began feeding corn cobs.
GEORGE: That was the cattle feeder involved with Kruschev?
ORVILLE: Yes, we went back and forth several times and got acquainted with Garst. We made more money feeding molasses, urea, and corn cobs to cattle than we ever did feeding dent corn. We used to feed 1,700 to 2,000 head of cattle every winter as a by product. We began to get cobs from anyone who was shelling either dent or popcorn. We would go get the cobs, haul them away and grind them for cattle feed.
GEORGE: So at that time McCarty had 16 Martin Ear Cribs and handling everything on the ear basis. Remember the tall crib McCarty built near Napoleon that Milt Sigg used to call the Tabernacle? Do you have any idea how much Popcorn that held?
ORVILLE: No, I don't.
GEORGE: The ones that we had ourselves held 600 tons in the pair, 300 tons to the side. But I think that thing was in to the multiple thousands. I can't recall whether that held 2,000 tons or not but I sort of suspect that it was close to that.
ORVILLE: It wasn't engineered strong enough. Remember they had to go in there and put old telephone poles up and brace it? It started to break out.
GEORGE: Not very many things, even when you use an engineer to help you, that are really strong enough to start with for storing heavy ear popcorn.
ORVILLE: That's one thing—those guys over at the mine. They built things heavy. Over built them. And then actually the iron looks like it was turned out by ore iron companies.
GEORGE: So then you were really commercially producing popcorn?
ORVILLE: The last year I was down there was in 1951 and we had 6,000 acres in popcorn.
GEORGE: 6,000 acres of ear popcorn?
ORVILLE: Not all was growing on Princeton Farms. These were contracted acres. We had some on Princeton Farms but we contracted with farms in Southern Indiana and over around Ridgeway, Illinois.
GEORGE: So you would have had probably 1,000 acres or 2,000 acres in Princeton's land at that time?

ORVILLE: I doubt. Because, see we were trying to run 600 acres of hybrid seed corn and didn't have popcorn yet. But we had to grow most of our popcorn off the Princeton Farms because I had my popcorn seed and my dent seed corn. And, of course, one of the advantages I had at Princeton farms was not having a scattered farm here and a farm there, so I could get a lot of isolation because it was not scattered.

GEORGE: So the part of the popcorn that you produced on that Princeton land would have been minor, 1,000 acres or so?

ORVILLE: I doubt if we had over 500 or 600 acres on our own farm.

GEORGE: For the entire setup. Wyandot never produced much popcorn on the Brown farm since the war time.

ORVILLE: We were producing seed wheat, producing soybean seeds and together with our dent seed corn. And then, see, we had a registered herd of Angus cattle and a registered herd of Hampshire hogs and Hampshire sheep and we showed them at state fairs. And then we fed some 2,000 head of cattle at that time.

GEORGE: So when you decided to go into the business with Charlie Bowman then, you had your own breeding work that you had been doing on popcorn.

ORVILLE: Both Charlie and I then had had about 11 years of experience in breeding popcorn seed. Charlie with Ag Alumni and I with Princeton Farms, so you see there is no chance for either one of us to go into ownership. Princeton Farms was a closed family corporation. No chance of ever buying there. And Charlie was working for Purdue University and no chance of buying there. And then when the seed corn plant, the dent seed corn plant, owned by George F. Chester and Son, southwest of Valparaiso was for sale, that's where we got the name Chester Hybrids. George F. Chester and Son, Dent Seed Corn Farm. They had been in business for 13 years, successful. His son was a Purdue graduate but he hurt his back and couldn't lift a bag of seed corn. So that's when he decided to sell that and they decided to come down to St. Petersburg and go in the motel business. Not George Chester, but his son did. George Chester still had his farm and he kept growing seed for us.

Appendix B

POPCORN RECIPES

All recipes courtesy of the Popcorn Board, www.popcorn.org.

Cranberry Almond Popcorn Muffins

Yield: 12 muffins

5 cups popcorn, popped
1½ cups flour
¼ cup sugar
1 tablespoon baking powder
½ teaspoon salt
½ cup dried sweetened cranberries
1 cup milk
1 egg
2 tablespoons vegetable oil
½ teaspoon almond extract
½ cup sliced almonds
¼ cup sugar mixed with 1 teaspoon cinnamon

Preheat oven to 400° Fahrenheit. Spray a 12-cup muffin pan with cooking spray or line with paper liners. Set aside.

Blend popcorn in a blender or food processor until finely ground. Pour ground popcorn into a large mixing bowl. Add flour, sugar, baking powder, salt and cranberries and stir until blended. Set aside.

Beat milk, egg, oil and almond extract together and pour over dry ingredients; stir just until combined. Spoon batter into muffin cups, filling each about half full.

Divide almonds among muffin tops and sprinkle with cinnamon sugar.

Bake 15 to 18 minutes or until tops are lightly browned. Serve warm with butter.

Cheesy Popcorn Bread

Yield: 9 squares

4 cups popcorn, popped
1 cup yellow corn meal
2 tablespoons sugar
2 teaspoons baking powder
½ teaspoon salt
1 egg
1 cup 2 percent milk
¼ cup vegetable oil
1 cup jack or pepper jack cheese, shredded
1 (4-ounce) can mild, diced green chilies, drained (optional)

Preheat oven to 400° Fahrenheit. Spray an 8-inch square baking pan with cooking spray. Set aside.

Process the popcorn in a blender or food processor until finely ground. Pour ground popcorn into a large bowl and stir in corn meal, sugar, baking powder and salt until blended.

Beat egg, milk and vegetable oil together in a small bowl and stir into popcorn mixture until just blended.

Scatter cheese and chilies, if desired, over batter and stir until just evenly distributed.

Pour batter into prepared pan and bake for 25 minutes or until lightly browned at edges and tester comes out clean. Cut into squares to serve.

Popcorn Pepperoni Pizza Dippers

Yield: 16 squares

2 eggs
½ cup Tomato and Basil Reduced Fat Cooking Crème
1 tablespoon Parmesan cheese, grated
1/8 teaspoon coarse ground black pepper
10 cups popcorn, popped
1 cup mozzarella cheese, shredded
⅓ cup thinly sliced pepperoni, coarsely chopped
Your favorite marinara sauce

Preheat oven to 350° Fahrenheit. Spray an 8-inch square baking pan with cooking spray.

Whisk together eggs, cooking crème, Parmesan cheese and black pepper in a large bowl. Stir in popcorn, mozzarella cheese and pepperoni. Spread mixture in prepared pan, patting down with a spatula or spoon.

Bake about 15 minutes until set and lightly browned. Let sit 5 minutes. Cut into 16 bars. Serve warm with marinara sauce.

Edible Popcorn Party Bowl

Yield: 1 bowl

10 cups popcorn, popped
1⅓ cups sugar
1 cup water
⅓ cup light corn syrup
½ teaspoon vinegar
¼ teaspoon salt
10 drops food color (optional)

Spray the inside of a large, stainless steel bowl with cooking spray and the outside of a second large, stainless steel bowl. Set aside. These 2 bowls will be used to form the popcorn bowl at the end of cooking time. (Note: If one bowl is smaller than the other, spray the outside of the smaller bowl.)

Spray a third large bowl with cooking spray and place popped popcorn inside. Set aside.

Stir sugar, water, corn syrup, vinegar and salt together in a medium saucepan. Bring mixture to a boil, cover and boil for 3 minutes to allow steam to wash down the sides of the pan. Remove lid and attach a candy thermometer to the pan.

Allow mixture to boil, without stirring, until it reaches 290° Fahrenheit. Stir in food color, if desired.

Working quickly, pour syrup over popcorn and toss with a large spoon until popcorn is thoroughly coated. Pour popcorn mixture into the first prepared bowl and use a spoon to push mixture evenly up onto the sides of the bowl.

Firmly press the second prepared bowl onto popcorn to form a popcorn bowl. Allow the popcorn bowl to cool completely between the stainless steel bowls.

To serve, tip popcorn bowl out and place on a platter. Fill with popcorn.

Popcorn Cereal Bowl

Yield: 1 bowl

Freshly popped popcorn makes a quick and delicious breakfast cereal. Popular in colonial America, popcorn for breakfast is fun and easy to prepare.

Place popcorn in a bowl and add cold milk, just like any breakfast cereal. Add a teaspoon or two of sugar (or cinnamon sugar) and your choice of the following stir-ins:

- dried fruit such as raisins, dates, apples and currants
- nuts, such as sliced almonds, toasted walnuts, pine nuts or pecan pieces
- fresh fruit such as sliced bananas, strawberries or raspberries
- tropical touches such as coconut flakes, dried papaya and pineapple pieces

Mix and match stir-ins. Create your own combinations!

Nacho-Cheese Popcorn

Yield: 2½ quarts

⅓ cup cooking oil
3 or 4 dried chilies
1 large clove garlic, cut into quarters
1 teaspoon cumin seed
⅓ cup popcorn, unpopped
3 tablespoons hot oil
⅓ cup Parmesan cheese
1 teaspoon paprika
½ teaspoon salt

Place cooking oil, chilies, garlic and cumin seed in a small saucepan. Cook over low heat for 3 minutes and then let stand for 10 minutes. Strain. Use 3 tablespoons of the seasoned oil for popping corn; reserve the rest.

This makes about 2½ quarts popped popcorn. Pour the remaining oil over popped popcorn, tossing to coat. Mix Parmesan cheese, paprika and salt. Sprinkle over popped popcorn, tossing to combine.

NOTES

Chapter 1

1. W. Hoover Brown, *Our Lives in Review* (Marion, OH: self-published, 1979).
2. Marion Area Chamber of Commerce, "Community Profile," http://www.marionareachamber.org/web_pages/community_profile.htm (accessed May 31, 2014).
3. Brown, *Our Lives in Review.*
4. Wyandot, Inc., "History of Our Snack Food Company," www.wyandotsnacks.com/our-company (accessed June 5, 2014).
5. Ibid.
6. Ibid.
7. C. Cretors and Co., "History," http://www.cretors.com/page.asp?i=12 (accessed June 4, 2014).
8. Wyandot Popcorn Museum, "History," http://www.wyandotpopcornmus.com/history.html (accessed May 31, 2014).
9. Andrew W. Smith, *Popped Culture: A Social History of Popcorn in America* (Columbia: University of South Carolina Press, 1999), 161.
10. John Jarvis, "ConAgra Foods Closing Plants," *Marion Star*, June 6, 2014, http://www.marionstar.com/apps/pbcs.dll/article?AID=2014306050019 (accessed June 16, 2014).

Chapter 2

11. Marion Area Chamber of Commerce, "Community Profile," http://www.marionareachamber.org/MarionCommunityProfile.pdf (accessed May 31, 2014).
12. J.W. Jacoby, *History of Marion County, Ohio and Representative Citizens* (Marion, OH: Marion County Historical Society, 1976), 52, 57, 59, 91, 140, 142–43.
13. National Parks Service, "Warren G. Harding Home," http://www.marionareachamber.org/web_pages/community_profile.htm.http://www.nps.gov/nr/travel/presidents/warren_harding_home.html (accessed May 31, 2014).

Chapter 4

14. Marion Popcorn Festival, *20th Anniversary Program* (Marion, OH: self-published, 2000).
15. Marion Popcorn Festival, *10th Anniversary Program* (Marion, OH: self-published, 1990).
16. Marion Popcorn Festival, *20th Anniversary Program.*
17. Ibid.
18. Ibid.
19. Marion Popcorn Festival, "Festival Main Stage Entertainment," http://www.popcornfestival.com/festival_main_stage_entertainmen.htm (accessed June 8, 2014).

Chapter 9

20. History.com, "Popcorn Was Popular in Ancient Peru, Study Suggests," http://www.history.com/news/popcorn-was-popular-in-ancient-peru-discovery-suggests (last modified January 20, 2012).
21. Ibid.
22. Popcorn Board, "Early Popcorn History/Recent Popcorn History," http://www.popcorn.org/EncyclopediaPopcornica/WelcometoPopcornica/HistoryofPopcorn/tabid/106/Default.aspx (accessed June 4, 2014).
23. Smith, *Popped Culture*, 53–54.
24. Ibid., 55–57.

25. Ibid., 58–59.
26. Ibid., 59–62.
27. Ibid., 62–65.
28. Popcorn Board, "Early Popcorn History."
29. Wyandot Popcorn Museum, "Holcomb & Hoke," http://wyandotpopcornmus.com/holcomb_and_hoke_history.html (accessed June 24, 2014).
30. Wyandot Popcorn Museum, "Burch and Manley," http://wyandotpopcornmus.com/burch_manley_history.html (accessed June 24, 2014).
31. Wyandot Popcorn Museum, "Paul Newman's Dunbar Model 11 Popcorn and Peanut Concession Wagon," http://wyandotpopcornmus.com/dunbar_history.html (accessed June 24, 2014).
32. Popcorn Board, "Recent Popcorn History."
33. Popcorn Board, "Industry Facts," http://www.popcorn.org/EncyclopediaPopcornica/WelcometoPopcornica/IndustryFacts/tabid/108/Default.aspx (accessed June 5, 2014).
34. Wyandot Popcorn Museum, "Popcorn History," http://wyandotpopcornmus.com/popcorn_history.html (accessed June 15, 2014).
35. Smith, *Popped Culture*, 163–64.
36. Popcorn Board, "Industry Facts."
37. Martha C. White, "A Snack Trend with Pop: Gourmet Popcorn Takes Over," *Time*, January 11, 2013, http://business.time.com/2013/01/11/a-snack-trend-with-pop-gourmet-popcorn-takes-over (accessed June 16, 2014).
38. American Chemical Society (ACS), "Popcorn: The Snack with Even Higher Antioxidants Levels than Fruits and Vegetables," ScienceDaily, www.sciencedaily.com/releases/2012/03/120325173008.htm (accessed June 16, 2014).
39. Smith, *Popped Culture*, xvii.

INDEX

ABOUT THE AUTHOR

Michelle "RJ" Rotuno-Johnson is a newspaper reporter who lives in Delaware, Ohio, with her fiancée and a small army of cats. She is a graduate of Ohio Wesleyan University and Roger Bacon High School (Cincinnati). When not writing books or newspaper articles, she enjoys cooking, singing barbershop, reading, playing video games and kicking around a soccer ball.

She is a fan of Chelsea FC, the United States national soccer team, the Boston Red Sox, the Columbus Crew and teams from her native Cincinnati. RJ is a proud member of Delta Zeta Sorority and Sweet Adelines International. She is also a member of Chelsea in America and of American Outlaws, the national USA soccer support group, and supports singer Miranda Lambert through the Ran Fans club.